Sleeping Dogs Don't Lay*

*and that's no lie

Also by Richard Lederer and Richard Dowis

The Write Way

Also by Richard Lederer

Basic Verbal Skills (with Phillip Burnham)
Anguished English
Get Thee to a Punnery
Crazy English
The Play of Words
The Miracle of Language
More Anguished English
Literary Trivia (with Michael Gilleland)
Building Bridge (with Arnold Fisher and Bo Schambelan)
Adventures of a Verbivore
Nothing Risqué, Nothing Gained
Pun & Games
Fractured English
The Word Circus

Also by Richard Dowis

How to Make Your Writing Reader-Friendly
The Lost Art of the Great Speech

Sleeping Dogs Don't Lay

Practical Advice for the Grammatically Challenged

Richard Lederer
and Richard Dowis

Illustrations by
Jim McLean

St. Martin's Griffin New York

 For information, address St. Martin's Press, 175 Fifth Avenue, New York, N.Y. 10010.

www.stmartins.com

The poem "An Ode to the Spell Checker" is used by permission of Jerrold H. Zar.

Design by Maureen Troy

Library of Congress Cataloging-in-Publication Data

Lederer, Richard.
Sleeping dogs don't lay : practical advice for the grammatically challenged / Richard Lederer and Richard Dowis.
p. cm.
Includes index.
ISBN 0-312-20363-2 (hc)
ISBN 0-312-26394-5 (pbk)
1. English language—Grammar Handbooks, manuals, etc. 2. English language—Rhetoric Handbooks, manuals, etc. I. Dowis, Richard. II. Title.
PE1112.L38 1999
428.2—dc21 99-27231
CIP

10 9 8 7 6 5 4

To my granddaughter, Jamie Kay Dowis, who, having lived in this grammatically challenged world for all of twenty-three months, has never made a grammatical error or committed a syntactical sin

—Richard Dowis

To my dog, Bart, who never lays

—Richard Lederer

Contents

Foreword, March!

Recently, scientists in India discovered a way to convert old newspapers into alcohol. The cellulose in the newsprint is broken down by a fungus into glucose and then fermented with yeast. Although they can't explain why, the inventors of the process have discovered that old copies of the upscale English-language daily *Hindustan Times* yield the most intoxicating results, more mind-spinning than the Indian-language newspapers.

These results do not surprise the authors of this book. We've long known that English is a truly intoxicating, mind-spinning language. English is also maddening, frustrating, exasperating, irritating, infuriating, vexatious, aggravating, troublesome, enraging, bothersome, riling, contradictory, flummoxing, and inefficient.

No language compares with English in wealth of words, shades of meaning, and degrees of diction. It comprises more words than any other of the world's hundreds of languages—six times as many as French, five times as many as Russian, four times as many as German—and it's growing. Spoken around the globe, English is increasingly the language of diplomacy, commerce, and technology.

But it is not an easy tongue. English is rife with irregularities, inconsistencies, and contradictions. In what other language can your nose run and your feet smell? In what other language can a woman be a vision but not a sight—unless your eyes are sore, in which case, she's a sight for sore eyes. No wonder many of us have trouble using our language correctly all the time.

Call us Ishmaels. Here we sit in the old crow's nest of the *Pequod,* the doomed whaling ship in Herman Melville's *Moby Dick,* nowadays the great ship of correct usage. Our vessel is marooned in the classroom and pocked by spitballs launched by today's youthspeak. Like, they go, "You know what we mean, duh? Whatever! Not!" Our ancient ship is tempest tossed by television, rammed by the media, and in danger of being dragged to the bottom by the Great White Whale of the Internet.

Rickety English pervades the speech and writing even of educated men and women. In videotaped testimony in the conspiracy trial of James and Susan McDougal and Arkansas governor Jim Guy Tucker, President Bill Clinton said, "Then after that, Mr. McDougal invited Hillary and I to invest with Jim and Susan in two-hundred and thirty acres in Marion County."

Now, President Clinton is no ignorant bumpkin. He is an educated, articulate man whose English is generally good. Yet more than once he has publicly erred by using a nominative pronoun as the object of a preposition. In that he's not by any means alone. In fact, Hillary Rodham Clinton similarly misfired in remarks at Lincoln Center: "It is a pleasure for the President, Vice President Gore, Mrs. Gore, and I to welcome . . ." Even professional writers make the same mistake. *Chicago Tribune* columnist Eric Zorn wrote, "The turn of the year is always a feast for we lovers of lists"; the high-priced news anchor Peter Jennings, of ABC, was heard to say, "Between he and Tsongas . . ."; and the unfailingly impeccable George Will showed a scintilla of peccability when he wrote about the death of Barry Goldwater: "It was a lot of fun for him and for we happy few who joined his parade."

Millions of people who *want* to speak and write correctly—and who usually do—make similar mistakes. Almost everyone must contend with at least one grammatical, syntactical, or word-use bugaboo—something he or she just can't seem to get right. A national food producer markets a cookie called "Bearwich's" and offers no reason for the apostrophe. A syndicated columnist admits he never knows when to use *whom*. A United States senator often says *infer* when he means *imply*. A respected college professor of our acquaintance has forgotten—if he ever knew—that *lay* is a transitive verb.

Which brings us to the title of this modest volume. Confusion of the transitive *lay* with the intransitive *lie* may well be the most common grammatical error the authors have encountered in our combined years of teaching, editing, and writing. And it was that error that inspired the title of this book, which we offer as a practical and often lighthearted look at some of the most common errors of English grammar and usage. *Sleeping Dogs* will serve the reader well as a quick-reference guide to preventing some of these errors. It is not intended to be a definitive book on writing and usage. For that, we recommend an earlier book on which we collaborated—*The Write Way* (Pocket Books, 1995).

Sleeping Dogs comprises (no, not *is comprised of*) ten chapters:

- I. Sleeping Dogs and Other Ponderables will help you find solutions to a number of enduring grammatical conundrums.
- II. Don't Bite Your Mother Tongue discusses some of the expressions that we recommend you use rarely, carefully, or never.
- III. Lightning Bugs and Lightning is a glossary of the most often abused and misused words and expressions in our language.
- IV. Things You *Know* That Just Ain't So takes you on a brief journey where sacred cows of grammar and usage are slaughtered (figuratively, of course) with impunity.
- V. Put Your Words in Order is a look at how careless arrangement of sentence elements (syntax) creates fuzzy and often hilarious writing.
- VI. Grammar Games invites you to take some humorous quizzes and, in the process, review many of the rules discussed in the first five chapters.
- VII. Help for the Orthographically Challenged offers some de-

vices to help you to be the most happy speller. This chapter concludes with a skills-enforcing quiz.

- VIII. The Common Comma and IX. Punctuation Perplexities clear up, without getting too technical, some of the questions you have about punctuation.
- X. A Ten-Minute Writing Lesson packs into ten suggestions, or principles, a lot of what the authors have learned about writing. You can immediately mine and cash in these golden nuggets and use them to improve your writing. In ten minutes? Well, allow us a little hyperbole. After all, we have spent an aggregate of more than three quarters of a century in the writing business, and we're still learning.

So, let's go forward from this Foreword and march along toward what we hope (no, not *hopefully*) will be an enjoyable and informative journey for you.

RICHARD LEDERER
San Diego, California

RICHARD DOWIS
Waleska, Georgia

I

Sleeping Dogs and Other Ponderables

"I don't want to talk grammar, I want to talk like a lady," says the irrepressible Eliza Doolittle in George Bernard Shaw's *Pygmalion*. Perhaps Miss Doolittle speaks for many who just don't want to bother with grammar but are quite eager to talk "like a lady"—or a gentleman. Or, for that matter, like a judge, a physician, or a corporate executive.

Using perfect grammar in speaking and writing does not necessarily mark one as articulate, clever, or even intelligent. It is quite possible to produce a sentence that is grammatically perfect but makes no sense. It is also possible to violate rules of grammar and still express yourself effectively, even eloquently, as boxing manager Joe Jacobs did when he shouted "We was robbed" in protest to what he thought was an unjust decision; or Elvis Presley when he crooned, "You ain't nothin' but a houn' dog"; or as did, on occasion, such luminaries as Shakespeare, Daniel Defoe, Lewis Carroll, and others.

Ralph Waldo Emerson made light of grammar when he wrote,

> Any fool can make a rule
> And every fool will mind it.

And the Holy Roman emperor Sigismund, when someone called to his attention a grammatical error he had made in a speech, said, "*Ego sum rex Romanus, et supra grammaticam*": "I am king of the Romans, and above grammar."

Even so, using bad grammar can mark a person as one who is careless of language and who may be, by extension, careless of other things. Most of us, most of the time, need to respect the rules and conventions of grammar. After all, a corporate CEO addressing shareholders, a judge charging the jury, or a physician writing for a medical journal can ill afford to sound like Joe Jacobs or Elvis Presley or be as arrogant as the Emperor Sigismund. Even in our era of film, television, computers, video games, and databases, the urge to put together a sentence correctly, sensibly, and even lovingly still engages the attention of many speakers and writers.

One place to start is to explain the title of this book.

Only wide-awake dogs can lay.

A *sleeping* dog cannot lay, but one that's wide awake can. How? By going for the newspaper and laying it at his master's feet.

To lay is to put something in place. *Lay* is a transitive verb, which means that it requires an object. A hen can lay an egg. A mason can lay bricks. A disciplinarian can "lay down the law." A child can correctly say, "Now I lay me down to sleep." It is incorrect to say *lay* unless you also say what is being laid. The *what* is the object of the verb *lay—egg, bricks, the law,* and *me* in the examples above.

Dave Martin, editor of *Kitplanes* magazine in San Diego, California, distributes a tongue-firmly-planted-in-cheek certificate to the negligent:

CONGRATULATIONS!

With this proclamation, you are recognized as a member of a none-too-exclusive group: recipients of the

Lie-Lay *Recognition Award*

Your award results from the incorrect use of the verb *lay* (infinitive form: *to lay*) in the following publication or broadcast: ______________

Through your own personal efforts (assuming some editor has not sabotaged your copy), you have demonstrated the common misunderstanding resulting in the misuse of the verb form to lie *that is noted among (1) folks in general, (2) most college graduates, (3) plenty of Ph.D.s, and (4) all too many professional broadcasters and writers.*

People don't lay *down; they* lie *down. And inanimate objects aren't capable of* laying *anything; they just* lie *there. On the other hand, chickens and stand-up comedians* lay *eggs, on purpose and accidentally.*

Considering all of this, we recommend that you ______________ *(pick one:* covet, treasure, trash, ignore*) this recognition that people really do read/listen to what you write and say.*

Again, our congratulations.

Note Dave Martin's claim that "people really do read/listen to what you write and say." Dramatic proof of that assertion is provided by Laura Miner, of Minneapolis. She tells us about her grandmother, who lived in a nursing home. When the elderly woman developed a serious fever, an ambulance was called. One of the crew asked the family, "Does she want to go laying down or sitting up?"

A member of the family suggested, "Why don't you ask Grandma?"

The ambulance crewman looked at the family with pity: "Surely you don't expect this ninety-plus elderly to be competent."

At which point nonagenarian Grandma said to the astonished crew, "*Laying down* is not correct grammar. It's *lying down*."

With eerie similarity, the *Toronto Globe and Mail* reported the story of an aged gentleman still sharp of mind: "At one hundred and four, when he collapsed during a round of golf, his wife said: 'Oh, George. Do you want to lay there a minute?' He opened his eyes and said, '*Lie* there,' before passing out again."

Do sleeping dogs lie or lay? Consider this letter to the authors from Mary Dillon, of Cumberland Center, Maine: "My friend Beth is a high-school English teacher and lives with her friend Sam, an intelligent Golden Retriever. One day, Beth's mother was riding in the backseat of the car with Sam, who insisted on leaning on Mother. Mother told Sam to 'lay down and behave.' No action. Mother repeated, 'Lay down, Sam.' Still no action. Beth turned and commanded, 'Lie down, Sam,' and down he went. He is, after all, the companion of an English teacher."

The principal parts of *to lay* are *lay* (present), *laid* (past), *laying* (present participle), and *laid* (past participle). Nonetheless, the prodigiously popular holiday doll, Sing and Snore Ernie, sings, snores, and slaughters the English language. At one point in his monologue, the sleepy Ernie says, "It feels good to lay down."

Ernie would be a far better example for American youth if he would study the correct usage in the following sentences:

The clerk saw the customer lay the money on the counter.

The customer laid the money on the counter.

The hen is laying two eggs daily.

The hen has laid two eggs daily for a month.

To lie means "to repose." *Lie* is intransitive, which means it does not take an object. It is often used with *down.*

Principal parts of *to lie* are *lie* (present), *lay* (past), *lying* (present participle), and *lain* (past participle). The following sentences are correct:

I often lie down for a nap after lunch.

Yesterday, I lay in bed for two hours after lunch.

I was lying down when the telephone call came.

I had lain there for only a few minutes when the phone rang.

If you have trouble keeping all these *lies* and *lays* straight, you have plenty of company—probably 100 million Americans and no telling how many foreign speakers of English. The main source of confusion is that the present tense of *to lay* is the same as the past tense of *to lie.* It is one of those anomalies that make the English language at once maddening and wonderful.

Is good grammar important to I?

We doubt that any reasonably literate person would ask the question that way. Yet we have often seen or heard from an educated person a sentence like "Is good grammar important to you and I?"

In an act of test-taking desperation, a student defined a pronoun as "a professional noun." The problem with many people is that they behave as amateurs when confronted with decisions about pronoun case.

In the irrepressible "Dilbert," the horn-haired boss says to Dilbert,

"Here's your new coworker Zimbu the Monkey. Zimbu learned English from the zoo keepers in a special program."

Dilbert frowns, "This monkey is an insult to the intelligence of the other workers and I!"

"Other workers and 'me,' not 'I,' " the monkey corrects.

What a difference the little word *and* makes! For a reason that has always been unclear, a sentence with a preposition or a verb requiring a compound object seems to throw many people for a proverbial loop. It's almost as if they can't decide whether the nominative or objective pronoun is required and so use one of each just to be safe. Here are some choice real-life examples:

- "What [he] was talking about was something that people like [Roger] Ailes and I are concerned with."—Political commentator Brit Hume, as quoted in the *San Diego Union*
- "Moakley reported assets for he and his wife of between $83,000 and $248,000. . . ."—from the *Boston Globe*
- "He was selling *Encyclopædia Britannica*, and he was telling my wife and I . . . that it was critical that we buy a set."—Howard Kleinberg, Cox Newspapers columnist
- "[A young woman dying of cancer] allowed a *Courier* photographer and I to chronicle her last days."—Garret Matthews, in *The Evansville* (Indiana) *Courier*
- "It was he and his wife's anniversary."—*The Ft. Lauderdale* (Florida) *Sun-Sentinel*

Would the perceptive and intelligent Brit Hume say "a person like *I*"? Would the *Globe* reporter write "assets for *he*"? Would Mr. Kleinberg say "he was telling *I*"? Would Garret Matthews write that the young woman "allowed *I* to chronicle"? Would the *Sun-Sentinel* reporter write "it was *he* anniversary"? Of course not. Yet these examples are real. The writers who made the errors experienced lapses of a type that is common to many professionals and amateurs, and they got no help from the newspapers' copy editors.

Don't let the pesky conjunction *and* trap you into saying or writing something as barbarous as "for he and I." Remember that *he* and *I* equals *us*. Think about it.

Halt! *Whom* goes there! Or does it?

Among the most nettlesome pronouns are *who* and *whom,* so much so that many would be happy to have *whom* excised from our language. That might happen someday, but for now we're stuck with the venerable pronoun and ought to use it correctly. The following sentence appeared in the *Atlanta Constitution:*

> "Two adults and two juveniles, including a sixteen-year-old whom investigators say was the trigger man, have been charged with the slaying of a convenience store clerk. . . ."

The writer of that sentence failed to apply either basic grammar or simple logic. *Whom* was the trigger man? Does *whom* go there? Of course not. Remove the parenthetical and irrelevant "investigators say" and the correct rendition becomes clear: "Two adults and two juveniles, including a sixteen-year-old who ~~investigators say~~ was the trigger man, have been charged. . . ."

The use of *whom* where *who* is required is a more egregious error than the use of *who* where *whom* is required and is more likely to be committed by educated people who usually speak and write correct English. The book *Shakespeare and the Jews,* by Edward Shapiro, professor of comparative literature at Columbia University, contains this sentence:

> At a time when many writers were trying to reinvent what it meant to be English, the English defined themselves by whom they were not.

The correct pronoun is *who,* as Professor Shapiro probably knows.

The same error is often committed by people who are trying hard to be correct but don't quite know how and think *whom* sounds more, well, refined. That is what Theodore Bernstein, the late assistant managing editor of the *New York Times,* called "overrefinement."

The grammar that governs the use of *who* and *whom* is fairly simple but is nonetheless confusing to some. *Who* is a nominative-case pronoun; *whom* is its objective-case counterpart. Other nominative/objective partnerships are *I/me, he/him, she/her, we/us,* and *they/them.* Use the nominative case for the subject of a verb, whether the verb is in a sentence or a clause. Use the objective for the object of a verb or the object of a preposition.

That's the grammatical explanation. If you're still in doubt whether to use a nominative or an objective pronoun, try the substitution method. Here's how it works: Instead of *who* or *whom,* insert some other pronoun. For instance, in the first example above, substitute the objective pronoun *him* for *whom:* "Two adults and two juveniles, including a sixteen-year-old *him* investigators say was the trigger man, have been charged. . . ." Then try it with *him*'s nominative counterpart, *he:* "Two adults and two juveniles, including a sixteen-year-old *he* investigators say was the trigger man, have been charged . . ."

Which sounds better? No contest. The second. Neither is correct, obviously, but "*him* [objective] was the triggerman" is jarring, while "*he* [nominative] was the triggerman" falls easily upon the ear. Therefore, you can readily tell that the nominative pronoun *who* is required: "Who investigators say was the triggerman. . . ."

Do not allow yourself to be misled by the way a sentence is put together. Think about what is being conveyed. Decide who is doing what to whom and the correct pronoun will probably become apparent.

Remember: It's not who you know; it's *whom* you know.

Let I do it? No, let me.

In Doug Marlette's "Kudzu" comic strip, one of the characters says, "Let he who is without sin cast the first stone." Wrong! The sentence is an ungrammatical misquotation of a biblical passage: "He that is without sin among you, let him cast the first stone." (John 8:7)

The misquotation itself is not especially egregious—it can be considered a paraphrase—but the grammatical error in it is. The correct version is "Let him who is without sin cast the first stone."

Atlanta Journal sports columnist Steve Hummer erred similarly when he wrote, "Pause for a moment to think about he who is not here." Errors of that kind are commonly made by writers whose grasp of the structure of a sentence is tenuous. In the biblical misquotation, remove the clause "who is without sin" and it becomes clear that "Let he cast the first stone" is incorrect. In Hummer's, remove "who is not here" and it becomes clear that "think about he" is incorrect.

A grammatical analysis of the misquotation shows that *let* is the sentence verb, with the unexpressed but understood *you* as its subject. *Let* is a transitive verb, and its object is *him,* which is why it must be an objective rather than a nominative pronoun. "Who is without sin" is a restrictive clause describing *him*.

The good news, though, is that you don't need all that heavy-duty grammatical analysis to choose the correct pronoun in either sentence. All you have to do is to break down the sentence into its elements and determine how they logically relate to each other. Then trust your ear—the same ear that will tell you that Marie Antoinette never commanded, "Let they eat cake!"

The smoking gun

Consider the following sentences:

> Smoking may be hazardous to your health.
>
> The investigators failed to find the smoking gun.

In each of the two, the verb *smoking* has a different function. It serves as a noun in the first and an adjective in the second. A verb form used as a noun is called a geru**N**d; a verb form used as an adjective is a p**A**rticiple. Therein is a clue to one of the most puzzling constructions in English. Clever fellows that we are, we have capitalized on your interest and boldly faced this issue by capitalizing and bold-facing the *N* in *gerund* and the *A* in *participle* to help you remember their respective parts of speech.

Which is correct?

The conductor disapproved of the tuba player chewing betel nut during the concert.

The conductor disapproved of the tuba player's chewing betel nut during the concert.

The correct choice is the second sentence, with the possessive noun *player's*. That's because *chewing*, a gerund, functions as the object of the verb phrase *disapproved of*. Similarly, "The conductor disapproved of his [not *him*] chewing betel nut" is preferred. The logic becomes clear when we think of it this way: What the conductor disapproved of was not the tuba player himself, but an *action* of the tuba player's—the infernal chewing.

"Mary dislikes John wearing a purple polka-dot shirt" seems to say that Mary dislikes John, but what Mary probably dislikes is the fact that John is wearing such a shirt. Presumably, she likes John just fine, even when he wears that abominable shirt. A subtle distinction, but a useful one.

Our recommendation: Make the noun or pronoun preceding a gerund possessive unless doing so would result in a confusing or an overly pedantic sentence.

Banishing the wicked *which*

One way to improve your writing is to go on a "*which* hunt" and excise any *which* that isn't "protected" by a comma and replace it with *that*. For example, if you find in the hunt that you have written "This is the automobile which I saw leaving the parking lot," change *which* to *that*.

Banishing the wicked which . . .

The use of *that* and *which* interchangeably to introduce relative clauses has a long history in our language and is especially common in the King James Bible. But most modern writers make a distinction between the two, and the distinction is useful because it helps to prevent ambiguity.

The rule to follow is this: When the relative clause is defining, restrictive, or essential, always use *that* and *never* precede it with a comma. When the relative clause is nondefining, nonrestrictive, or nonessential, introduce it with *which* and precede it with a comma.

In "I plan to wear the blue suit that I bought at Macy's," the clause "that I bought at Macy's" is restrictive (or defining) because it designates one particular suit. The speaker might have any number of blue suits, but the one she plans to wear came from Macy's. In "I plan to wear my blue suit, which I bought at Macy's," the clause "which I bought at Macy's" simply gives a nonessential additional fact, almost an afterthought, about the suit. It implies that she has only one blue suit.

An even simpler guide is "With a comma, use *which;* with no comma, use *that.*"

Double negatives are no-no's.

No speaker of standard English would say, let alone write, "I haven't got no money." That's because, as any schoolchild knows, English—unlike some other languages—does not permit double negatives. "I have NOT got NO money" is about as "double negativish" as it gets.

Even so, a "milder" form of double negative is distressingly common in the speech and writing of educated people. On a baseball broadcast, the play-by-play announcer said, "I haven't seen him throw hardly any curve balls today." Wrong! Doubly wrong! Adverbs such as *scarcely, only, but,* and *hardly;* pronouns like *no one* and *nothing;* and the conjunctions *neither* and *nor* are all negative in effect and should not be used with other negatives.

Another fairly common example of a double negative is "I wouldn't be surprised if she didn't show up unannounced" when the speaker obviously means "I wouldn't be surprised if she showed up unannounced."

An especially egregious double negative results when a writer or speaker attempts to make an already negative word "more negative": "We will go irregardless of the weather"; "The men unloosened their ties." People who say things like that just ain't got no couth.

A type of double negative that is acceptable is one in which the second negative is almost an afterthought, as in the children's song about George Washington: "I will not lie / Oh, no, not I / Not even if I catch it." Using a double negative is also correct when one negative word or phrase is intended to cancel the other: "Not for nothing was George Washington called 'the Father of our Country' "; "This is not an unimportant point."

Although English frowns on the double negative, it tolerates—and in some cases requires—the double possessive. "A picture of him" is not the same as "a picture of his," but "a friend of the president" means the same as "a friend of the president's," and both are correct. We can say "a friend of his," but "a friend of him" is incorrect unless it appears in a sentence like "I am a friend of him who is an enemy of my enemy."

The subject of the double possessive (or double genitive, as it is sometimes called even though *genitive* is a slightly broader term than *possessive*) is replete with subtleties. It is not, however, a subject that requires a long discussion here, because errors in the use of possessives are almost nonexistent. In virtually every instance, the ear is a reliable guide.

An agreeable subject

A correspondent asks which of the following sentences is correct:

All she ever wears is dresses.
All she ever wears are dresses.

This kind of construction puzzles many people, but the answer is simple: The subject of the sentence is *all,* which is a singular pronoun even though what it represents (dresses) is plural. *Dresses* is a predicate nominative or, as it is sometimes called, the subject complement. Since the subject, not the complement, controls the verb form and *all* is singular, the construction requires the singular verb *is.* Hence, the first sentence is the correct one.

If we reverse the order of the sentence elements and make *dresses* the subject, *all* becomes the complement. The plural verb form is then required: "Dresses are all she ever wears."

Similarly, when *what* is the subject of a sentence, it is treated as singular even when the "what" being discussed is plural. Example: "What I like most about summertime is fresh vegetables."

A good reminder is the novelty song "All I Want for Christmas Is My Two Front Teeth." Think of that when you're tempted to write "All she ever wears are dresses" or "My favorite dessert are doughnuts."

Collective guilt?

The leader of the writing seminar asks, "Which is correct, 'The couple *was* married five years ago' or 'The couple *were* married five years ago'?"

Immediately from the participants comes a chorus of "Was!"

"Right," the leader says. "Now, how about 'The couple was married five years ago, but now it is divorced and living in separate apartments'?"

No chorus this time. Just puzzled looks. It might be acceptable (barely) to say the couple is divorced, but to say "it" is living in separate apartments is absurd. So, is *couple* singular or is it plural? The answer is "yes." That is, it can be either.

Certain nouns are singular in form but may be either singular or plural in concept. Among them are *couple, family, group, staff, majority, team, jury, total, number,* and *committee.* Such words are called collectives. The list is long. The question often arises whether to treat a collective, grammatically, as singular or plural—in other words, which verb form to use with it.

Most of the time (in the United States, but not in Britain), collectives are treated as singular, but, as with many grammatical questions, function rather than form is the more important consideration. Simply stated, this means that what the writer has in mind should be the controlling factor. For instance, in a sentence such as "A majority of the voters in the district (is/are) Republicans," the word *majority* clearly means "most" and thus requires the plural verb *are.*

Although, as we have previously stated (see "An agreeable subject," above), the subject of the sentence determines the verb form, this is an instance in which the complement *(Republicans),* being plural, reinforces the plural verb. In "A majority of the voters in the district is Republican," the writer is thinking of the majority as a group rather than as individual voters. The fact that the complement *(Republican)* is singular provides reinforcement.

Number and *total* offer interesting examples. "The number of employees has increased since last year," but "A number of employees have more than ten years with the company." Similarly, "The total is larger than in previous years," but "A total of ten people are enrolled in the seminar." In these examples, the controlling words are *the* and *a.* With *the,* treat the collective as singular; with *a,* treat it as plural.

No one need worry about collective guilt. The best way to determine which verb form to use with a collective is to ask yourself what you want to say. Most of the time, the correct verb will be evident. If it isn't, the difference probably will not be worth bothering about.

Just one of those things

Several years ago *McCall's* magazine published an advertisement with a headline describing an attractive young woman as "One of the drab homebodies who *reads* [our emphasis] McCall's." A Chicago advertising executive wrote a letter to *Ad Age,* the advertising trade journal, taking issue with the copywriter's use of *reads,* claiming the correct word to be *read:* "One of the drab homebodies who read McCall's." The letter elicited a flood of others from *Ad Age* readers who weighed in on one side or the other. *Ad Age* called the controversy "the Great McCall's Grammar Debate."

The question comes up from time to time and always seems to generate a lot of discussion and disagreement. William Safire, the *New York Times* columnist and self-described language maven, wrote, " 'Conduct unbecoming an officer and a gentleman' is one of those phrases that sounds as if it comes out of Kipling." In a later column, Safire told of being excoriated by readers for using *it comes* instead of *they come.*

So who was right, Safire or his critics? The Chicago ad exec or the *McCall's* copywriter? Safire and *McCall's* were wrong. (Safire, by the way, acknowledged the error. As far as we know, *McCall's* remained silent, enjoying the free publicity.)

What both Mr. Safire and the copywriter failed to consider is that the sentence dealt with both plural and singular—the group and one member of the group: A number of phrases [the group] *sound* as if *they come* from Kipling; "Conduct unbecoming an officer and a gentleman" [the single member] *is one of them.* A number of drab homebodies [the group] *read McCall's;* the young woman [the single member] in the ad *is one of them.*

Wilson Follett, in *Modern American Usage,* expressed it this way:

"Order, reasoning, is sidetracked again in the construction that we may call the *one-of-those-who-is* blunder, probably the commonest in speech and print alike, in spite of being one of the most easily detected. *He is one of those who fights back:* the orderly mind sees where the singular statement about the individual ends, where the plural statement about the group or class begins, and such a mind avoids mixing the forms. But to see such matters one has to look. The many who never think of looking have sprinkled millions of lines with *those who fights, prophets who goes unrecognized, children who has never known parental companionship, peaks that wears a perpetual crown of snow,* and so on without end."

Our advice: When you begin a sentence with "one of those," don't automatically assume that *one* governs every verb in the sentence. Think.

Are two heads better than one?

"Members of the city council," wrote the editor of a daily newspaper, "really have their heads on straight." Whoa! How many heads does each councilor have? Shouldn't the sentence read, "Members of the city council really have their head on straight"? On the other hand, is there one giant head shared by all? How about "The teacher asked her students to raise their hands if they needed help"? Did she mean for each student to raise both hands? Unlikely.

Many grammar and usage manuals don't address this puzzler, perhaps because English has no definitive rule to guide a writer in making the correct choice. Nevertheless, your intrepid coauthors will give it a whirl.

In most instances, the number (singular or plural) of nouns or pronouns should be consistent throughout the sentence. Therefore, the plural *heads* is the correct choice in the first sentence quoted above. In the second sentence, however, the better choice is *hand* because *hands* is ambiguous unless there was a possibility that the teacher wanted the students to raise both hands. The singular is usually acceptable, and sometimes preferred, when only one of the thing in question could belong to each person. In "The senator knew thousands of constituents by their first (name/names)," the singular seems better, but either is acceptable.

Another exception is allowed for certain idiomatic expressions, such as "The men were told to let their conscience [not *consciences*] be their guide [not *guides*]," and for abstract or intangible nouns: "Members of Congress have changed their mind [not *minds*] about the legislation"; "On Black Friday, many ruined investors jumped to their death [not *deaths*]."

It should be obvious, but evidently it isn't, that when "ownership" of the thing in question is shared by the group, the singular is correct. For example, "The members of the team did not want reporters in their locker room." An *Atlanta Journal* article included these sentences: "Left out of negotiations about a proposed settlement with Big Tobacco, farmers who depend on the crop for their *livelihoods* worry about their *futures*. Many have tried alternative crops, but have been unable to shake their *dependency* on tobacco [emphasis added]."

If *livelihoods* and *futures* are plural, why isn't *dependency*? It seems to us that all three should be singular because all three are shared by the group and are also intangibles.

When all's said and done, the ear and common sense may be the best guide [*guides*?].

On the subject of subjects

The *Atlantic City Press* reported that "one in five adults don't know how to use a road map." In the *Scrivener,* a publication of The American Society of Writers on Legal Subjects, appeared this sentence: "Each of us owe her a debt of gratitude." From an article in the sports section of the *New York Post,* we learn that "the Nets' seven owners are meeting this afternoon, but determining the fates of Beard and GM Willis Reed are not on the agenda."

Those three sentences have one thing in common: They violate a fundamental principle of sentence construction. If you didn't detect the errors on first reading, reread the sentences, which is exactly what the writers should have done.

The violated principle is that a subject must agree with its verb in number. In the first sentence, the subject is *one,* not *adults,* and requires the singular verb form *doesn't.* In the second, the subject is *each,* which is singular and takes *owes* as its verb. In the third, the subject of the dependent clause is the gerund *determining,* which is singular and requires the singular verb *is.* In all three the writer evidently was thrown off course by the words that separate the subjects from the verbs.

No reasonably literate person violates the principle of subject-verb agreement when the subject and verb are side by side. Surely the *Press* reporter would not write "one adult don't know how to use a road map." Nor would the *Scrivener* writer say, "Each owe her a debt of gratitude." But when the subject and verb are separated by a few words, many writers and speakers seem to lose their way and the subject. Errors of this kind are common, but they are easy to avoid by the simple device of thinking what is being said.

Here are a few more things worth remembering about subject-verb agreement:

1. With a compound subject joined by *and,* use a plural verb: "Juanita and Tomás are from San Antonio."

2. With a compound subject joined by *or,* let the subject element closer to the verb determine the verb form: "The girl or the boys are bringing the picnic lunch," but "The boys or the girl is bringing the picnic lunch."

3. When two parts of a compound subject are thought of almost as one, use a singular verb form: "Ice cream and cake was served at the party." "Ice cream and cake *were* served. . . ." implies a separateness that seems unwarranted, but the compound subject "hot dogs and hamburgers" rates a plural verb because the two items are distinctly different.

4. When a subject contains both a positive and a negative element, the positive element determines the choice of verb even if it is not closer to the verb: "The dog, not the horses, was our main concern"; "The horses, not the dog, were our main concern."

What shall we do about *shall*?

When General Douglas MacArthur, forced by Japanese advances to depart the Philippines for Australia in March 1942, uttered his famous "I shall return," just what was he saying? Was he making a simple statement about the future, or was he *vowing* to return?

A reasonable inference is that the general was making a vow to return victorious, and that is certainly how history has interpreted the statement. But by traditional grammar he was simply revealing an intention. That's because the usage as it once was taught in elementary school required that simple futurity in the first person singular and plural (*I, we*) be expressed by *shall* and in the second and third persons singular and plural (*you, he, she, it, they,* and *y'all*) by *will*. So by tradition, MacArthur should have said "I will return" to express the determination he no doubt intended.

The traditional distinction between *shall* and *will* is still observed to some extent in Britain but to a much lesser extent in the United States. "In current American speech," wrote Bergen and Cornelia Evans in *A Dictionary of Contemporary American Usage* (1957), "*will* occurs 217 times for every *shall*. . . ."

So, what *shall* we do about *shall*? Well, unless we're lawyers, we will probably forget about it. In a legal document, *shall* expresses a mandate, as in "The party of the first part shall" do so and so. And, of course, *shall* is still required in questions such as "Shall we go on to something more important?"

Yes, let's.

Time is of the essence.

In an article about the search for Eric Rudolph, the survivalist suspected of bombing a clinic in Birmingham, *Newsweek* wrote: "Investigators got a break last week when they found a truck, believed to be stolen by Rudolph. . . ." Because the alleged theft was a completed, or "perfected" event, the phrase should have been "believed to have been stolen." The error is not uncommon. (And that last sentence is an acceptable double negative.)

English verbs have three basic tenses—present, past, and future. To each tense designation can be added "perfect" to express a completed ("perfected") action, often with an auxiliary such as *have*. Thus, *run* (present) becomes *have run* in the present perfect; *ran* (past) becomes *had run* in the past perfect; and *will run* (future) becomes *will have run* in the future perfect. A "perfect" tense signifies that an action has been completed (present perfect), had been completed before the present (past perfect), or will have been completed after some specified time in the future (future perfect).

Using tenses properly will not be troublesome if you stop to think about the action of each verb and determine when the action took or takes place. Keeping tenses in the proper relationship with each other is called sequence of tenses. These are examples of sentences with correct sequence of tenses:

When she retired [past], she had worked [past perfect] for the company fifty years.

She will retire [future] on July 1 and will have worked [future perfect] for the company fifty years.

She worked [past] fifty years with the company and has just retired [present perfect].

Differences in meaning reflected in tense can be subtle. Consider these three sentences:

She would like to have gone to the party.
She would have liked to go to the party.
She would have liked to have gone to the party.

The first sentence means that in the present the speaker wishes she had gone to the party. The second means that at some time in the past, she wanted to go to the party. We often hear sentences similar to the third one, but we are hard pressed to think of a situation that would call for a construction like that.

In a sentence with a dependent clause, the verb in the dependent clause should be the same tense as the verb of the main clause. A common error is a shift to the present tense in a dependent clause when the verb of the main clause is in the past. Example: "The chairman told the shareholders that earnings for the year will increase by 15 percent." Standard English and stylish writing require that the verb in the dependent clause be *would increase*. Failing to adhere to this rule, however, is not an especially egregious error, and few grammarians would find serious fault with *will increase* in the sentence. In any case, the rule is usually not followed when an axiom, a universal truth, or a scientific fact is expressed. Example: "In General Science class, the pupils learned that the sun is [not *was*] 93,000,000 miles from Earth."

We beg to differ.

"Basketball players are different than you and me. For one thing they are a lot taller," writes a reporter in the *San Diego Union-Tribune.*

That should be "different from you and me," in part because the writer is alluding to F. Scott Fitzgerald's "The rich are very different from you and me."

Why? Read on.

Which of the following pair of sentences is correct?

> Eva's recipe for Hungarian goulash is different from Zsa Zsa's.
> Eva's recipe for Hungarian goulash is different than Zsa Zsa's.

This construction puzzles many writers. Let's call it the "*different from/different than* conundrum." To explain the solution, we will review a principle that most of us learned in grammar school:

English adjectives and adverbs take three forms—positive, comparative, and superlative. The positive form is the basic one—a *good* book, for example. The comparative form, as the name implies, is used to compare *one* thing with another—a *better* book. The superlative form compares one thing with *more than one* of the same group or category—the *best* book of the three. With a few exceptions ("put one's best foot forward," "the *New York Times* Best Sellers"), the superlative should not be used when only two things are involved. Thus, it is not correct to say or write, "This is the best of the two books Lederer and Dowis have coauthored."

The comparative form is often used with *than*. For example, "This novel is better than the one I read last week." In fact, the conjunction *than* is used almost exclusively with comparative forms of modifiers.

Now, back to the *different from/different than* conundrum. In "Eva's recipe for Hungarian goulash is different than Zsa Zsa's," no comparison is expressed, because *different* is one of those adjectives that have no degrees. There are no such words as *differenter* and *differentest,* and even *more different* and *most different* are at best shaky concepts. (You would not say or write, for example, that Eva's recipe is "more different than Zsa Zsa's.") Therefore, because *than,* as we have noted, is used almost exclusively with comparatives, the second sentence, "Eva's recipe for Hungarian goulash is different than Zsa Zsa's," is the incorrect one.

Another way to look at it is to convert in your mind's eye the adjective *different* to the verb *differs,* from which *different* derives. Clearly, then, "Eva's recipe differs from Zsa Zsa's" is correct. "Eva's recipe differs than Zsa Zsa's" makes no sense.

It is permissible to use *than* with *different* when an adjective clause follows, as in "The meaning of this word is different than it was in Shakespeare's time." Some purists would not allow even that exception and would instead advise recasting the sentence to something like "The meaning of this word is different today from its meaning in Shakespeare's time," but we feel that the exception is reasonable.

So, *Sleeping Dogs*' advice is this: When you're confronted with the choice between *different from* and *different than,* make *different from* your first choice. You'll almost always be right. But if your ear tells you otherwise, choose *different than.*

Comparison proves . . . sometimes.

One of the most common errors we encounter is one that grammarians call "false comparison," comparing two things that cannot logically be compared. For example, "Prices are not as high in Germany as France" makes an illogical comparison between *prices* and *France.*

The problem is easily solved by inserting *in* before *France,* which gives us a sentence that is elliptical for "Prices are not as high in Germany as *they are in* France."

Although false comparisons usually do not cause misunderstanding, they can. "The employee's view, like the manager, was not relevant to the decision" leaves the reader wondering whether it was the manager herself or the manager's view that was irrelevant.

Most false comparisons are the result of hasty writing in which the writer has carelessly omitted a word or two. This should not be confused with ellipsis, which is the permissible and often desirable omission of one or more words. Whether they cause misunderstanding or not, false comparisons do not belong in polished writing.

Beware of sloppy drinking.

Careless speakers and writers often omit words that ought not to be omitted. Even an omission that does not result in misunderstanding may rob writing of style and grace. For example, a sentence such as "He will or already has mailed a check" would not likely be misunderstood, but the omission of *mail* after *will* offends the sensitive ear because when we eliminate the parenthetical "or already has" we have an inappropriate pairing of the future tense *(will)* and the past tense *(mailed):* "He will mailed a check."

A sentence like "The reporter was fired for sloppy work and drinking" is good for a chuckle because it leaves open to question the reporter's fastidiousness as a drinker. Presumably, the writer intended to say, "The reporter was fired for sloppy work and for drinking." It is one of the many peculiarities of English that reversing the order of the complaints against the reporter makes the second *for* unnecessary and leaves the intended meaning intact. "He was fired for drinking and sloppy work" is perfectly clear and acceptable.

Of course, certain words can be omitted to good effect. For instance, in "To err is human; to forgive, divine," repetition of the verb *is* would weaken the sentence. An omission of that type is a rhetorical device called syllepsis. In "Michael Jordan is taller than Shannon Miller," tacking *is* or even *is tall* onto the end of the sentence is unnecessary to either clarity or correct grammar. It is important, however, to think *is tall.* Otherwise there is the temptation to write abominations like "He is taller than her" rather than "He is taller than she [is tall]."

Have you a datum I can use?

The controversy rages: Is *data* singular or plural? On the one hand are the purists, who insist it is plural; on the other are the modernists, who say purists are transplants from the eighteenth century, and that *data* is a synonym for *information* and is therefore clearly singular. So which camp are we in? Is *data* singular or plural? The answer is yes. That is, it can be either, depending partly on your preference and partly on what you want to say or emphasize. Let's explore the subject so you can decide for yourself.

Technically, at least, the purists are right: *data* is the plural of the Latin word *datum. Datum,* however, is rarely used except in scientific or academic writing. We daresay the typical educated American is only vaguely aware of the word, if at all. So if we insist that *data* is always plural, we have a word that, for most practical purposes, has no singular.

Our friend Norm Storer, a writer from San Diego, composed this limerick to poke good-natured fun at the purists:

Consider the Latin word *data,*
As common as "French fried potata";
  It's used around town
  As a singular noun—
Except by some Kappas (Phi Beta).

The modernists have a good point. Most of the time, *data* is meant to be a synonym for *information,* a collection of facts. It seems reasonable to say, "There is sufficient data [information] to support the conclusion." It also seems reasonable to say, "These data [items of information] support the conclusion."

Our own bent, owing to early schooling, is to use *data* as plural most of the time, but if you prefer it as singular all, most, or some of the time, you have our blessing.

Much ado about sexism

Traditional English requires a masculine pronoun or pronominal adjective *(he, him, or his)* with a singular antecedent when the sex of the antecedent is unspecified. "A doctor must respect *his* patients if *he* wants them to respect *him*" is correct—by traditional rules—even though a doctor can be either a woman or a man. Those who defend traditional usage say that *his, he,* and *him* are not gender specific when used in that way. Those who believe it is time to scrap traditional usage counter that it perpetuates the myth of male superiority. They also contend, not without justification, that using masculine pronouns implies that some professions are exclusively for men, others for women.

Consider what happens when you substitute *nurse* for *doctor* in the example above: "A nurse must respect *his* patients if *he* wants them to respect *him*." Doesn't sound right, does it? That's because the vast majority of nurses are women. But there are many male nurses, and there are many female doctors. Until recently, most writers would have thought nothing amiss about the sentence with *doctor,* but they invariably would have written "A nurse must respect *her* patients. . . ." instead of "A nurse must respect *his* patients. . . ."

Stereotypes die hard. A woman wrote: "I just attended a charity brunch. The speaker was a prominent physician who happens to be a woman. After the emcee told us about her grants and studies and awards, he added, to everyone's horror, 'On top of that, she's got great legs.' A hiss went through the room."

Such boorishness, of course, deserves a hiss and more, but does it have anything to do with the subject at hand—writing the English language?

To the extent that our use of language perpetuates such stereotypes, yes. The practice of using the masculine pronoun to include both male and female, and the use of certain words that imply masculinity when what they refer to could be either male or female, has been condemned as "sexist" writing. We are sensitive to such concerns and we believe all writers should be. Clearly, sexist writing offends a significant number of people and ought to be avoided.

Still, we are equally aware that a significant number are offended by what they see as debasement of the language in the name of political correctness. We have no desire to become entangled in that debate. Our purpose is to offer readers of *Sleeping Dogs* some guidance in how to write clearly and correctly without offending either group. Is that possible? Read on.

Is tedium a sexually transmitted disease? Some writers, in a misguided effort to be oh, so modern and politically correct, resort to all manner of machinations to avoid "sexist" writing. This effort often shows up in the unremitting use of such locutions as *he or she, himself/herself,* and even *him/herself* to avoid the universal *he* or *him* as a reference pronoun when the sex of a singular antecedent is unknown or unspecified.

"A doctor must respect his or her patients" seems innocuous enough, but a little *his or her* can go too far. The true zealot continues with "A doctor must respect his or her patients if he or she wants them to respect him or her." That's when tedium sets in. And it just might be a fatal disease.

The problem is that the English language has no suitable pronoun for use when the sex of a subject can be either male or female. If we had the power, we would simply decree that the language provide a pronoun that would mean either *he* or *she*. But we haven't such power, and language just doesn't work that way.

The problem didn't begin with the feminist movement. It has been recognized, and solutions sought for it, since at least the nineteenth century. One suggested neutral pronoun, *thon,* never caught on, but it remained in some dictionaries until the 1950s. Other rejected suggestions include *co, E, mon, heesh, na, hir,* and *pa.* One university press published a book using *hir.*

We strongly recommend against using the ungainly *him/her, himself/herself,* and *him/herself,* and the nonwords *theirself* and *themself.* The following appeared in a telephone company booklet on handling obscene calls: "Hang up if the caller doesn't say anything . . . or if the caller doesn't identify themself."

We are dubious also about the merit of alternating the masculine and feminine pronouns, a device we have seen from time to time. This device is too contrived. We want readers to enjoy what we write, not to be concerned with whether one sex gets more mentions than the other.

Sexually transmitted tedium also shows up in the indiscriminate use of words purported to replace "noninclusive" terms for certain jobs and professions. We have not yet come to terms with *busser* and *waitron,* but *server* seems to us to be perfectly serviceable. We happily accept *letter carrier* for *mailman* and *flight attendant* for *stewardess.* Indeed, we feel privileged to live in an age when a flight attendant can make a pilot pregnant.

Is there a natural solution? When the reference is clearly to more than one person, perhaps the most natural solution is to toss traditional grammar out the window and use *they, them,* or *their* when you need a singular, genderless pronoun or pronominal adjective. Thus, "Everyone must do his own work" becomes "Everyone must do their own work." Purists may become apoplectic upon reading this, but the construction is almost universal in educated speech and increasingly common in writing. For some years now, we have been seeing it in well-edited publications such as the *New York Times* and the *Wall Street Journal.* Moreover, the sense of *everyone* (read, "all people") is plural even though the word is technically singular.

If you are bothered by the pairing of the technically singular pronoun *everyone* with the plural pronominal adjective *their*, just remember two things: First, English is replete with contradictions. They are called idioms—expressions that are accepted as correct but do not follow the usual grammatical rules. Second, when there is a conflict between grammar and common usage, grammar always loses in the long run. As our language evolves, the meanings of plural pronouns such as *they* and *their* almost certainly will expand to embrace the singular, just as *you* embraces both singular and plural today.

Are we ready to recommend, without reservation, the *everyone-their* solution? No, but we cannot condemn its use in most informal speech and writing.

A word of caution: If you choose the natural solution, do not fall into the trap of using the plural pronoun when the antecedent is singular and its sex is clear, as TV personality Oprah Winfrey has been known to do: "One question a mother should ask a baby-sitter when they leave them with their child . . ." Of the three pronouns, two refer to *mother,* one to *baby-sitter*. Although we cannot assume a baby-sitter to be female, we think it is safe, even in these days of medical miracles, to assume that a mother is a female.

The best solution—the way to avoid sexism, tedium, and even the appearance of bad grammar—is to recast the sentence. The downside of this is that recasting denies a writer some flexibility. In some instances, though, recasting improves the sentence while it solves the sexism problem.

Here are some different ways to recast sentences:

- *Drop the "his."* In "The employer withholds the money from his employees' paychecks and transfers it to the United Way," *his* serves no purpose. Eliminating it makes a better sentence. "The employer withholds the money from employees' paychecks and transfers it to the United Way."

- *Convert to plural.* It is often a simple matter to change the sentence to plural, thus eliminating the need for a singular pronominal adjective: "A doctor must respect his patients if he wants them to respect him" becomes "Doctors must respect their patients if they want their patients to respect them."
- *Change "his" to "the."* "Every account executive will submit a report to his client regularly" can just as easily be "Every account executive will submit a report to the client regularly."
- *Use a noun.* "We are hoping to find a tennis professional to put on a demonstration. After the demonstration, we'd like him to give tips to individual members of the club" can be stated effectively as "We are hoping to find a tennis professional to put on a demonstration. After the demonstration, we'd like the pro to give tips to individual members of the club."
- *Use second person pronouns.* When appropriate, the second person *you* or *your* makes the communication more personal and can eliminate the need for the third person *his*. With this recasting, "Each employee must turn in his time sheets by five P.M. Friday" becomes "You must turn in your time sheets by five P.M. Friday."

With a little thought, you will be able to come up with alternatives to gender-specific nouns and pronouns. Try it, you might even come to like it.

II

Don't Bite Your Mother Tongue

When teaching and writing about writing, we occasionally find it useful to be *proscriptive* rather than *prescriptive,* which is to say to tell students or readers what *not* to do rather than what to do. This can be a precarious undertaking, because opinions on such matters as diction vary widely, or to put it another way, one man's fish is another man's *poisson*.

Take, as an example, the word *alright*. Some dictionaries now tell us that *alright* is an acceptable variation of *all right*. We disagree. Does this mean that we think the dictionaries are "alwrong" about *alright* and that people who write "alright" are "alwet"? Not exactly.

Modern dictionaries are increasingly descriptive. In other words, they provide us with a picture, or description, of the language without being especially judgmental about what is right and what is wrong. It's like a photograph of a man with a double chin: The photo may be an accurate portrayal of the man, but that doesn't mean double chins are desirable as distinguishing features.

There is no doubt that *alright* has become relatively common, especially in informal writing. In that sense, it belongs in the dictionary's picture of the American language. Nevertheless, our position is that *alright* is unacceptable because the most qualified arbiters of our language say so. Not many good writers write *alright*, and no good copy editor of our acquaintance allows it to slip by.

Eighty-six percent of a panel of distinguished writers and other professional communicators assembled by William and Mary Morris as consultants for their *Dictionary of Contemporary Usage* disapproved of *alright* as the equivalent of *all right*. We must point out, brilliant mathematicians that we are, that this left 14 percent of those distinguished men and women who thought *alright* to be all right. So we can reasonably extrapolate that a similar percentage might disagree with many of the other positions we are about to take in this discussion.

And speaking of distinguished men, the avuncular Walter Cronkite has observed, "[F]or those who speak and write formally—presumably setting the standards of proper usage—there must be exercised the utmost care to prevent debasement of the language through too hasty acceptance of the vernacular." Amen to that!

With these thoughts in mind, we will undertake to persuade you to think as we do about the words and phrases presented here, to regard them as words and phrases to use sparingly, if at all, and correctly (carefully), if at all. We have designated each as *never, sparingly,* or *carefully.*

accidently (never)
This is a misspelling of *accidentally,* but it seems to be knocking on the door of respectability. In speech it can be passed off as sloppy pronunciation, but not in writing. The point to be made is that the adverb is not constructed by adding *ly* to the noun *accident;* it is formed by adding the adverbial suffix to the adjective *accidental.*

an historic (never)
"This is an historic occasion," intoned Senator Pfogbottom.

"I don't care to listen to this windbag," said the cynical reporter. "I think I'll go to McDonald's for an hamburger."

The rule is that *a* is used with words that begin with consonant *(a, e, i, o, u) sounds, an* with vowel *sounds.* We have emphasized *sounds* because the initial sound, not the initial letter, determines whether to use *a* or *an.* When the *aitch (h)* is silent, as in *honor* and *hour,* use the article *an.* When the *aitch* is pronounced, as in *house, hamburger, history,* and *historical,* use the article *a.*

and/or (sparingly)
This fairly recent device has a certain appeal to those who value utility above all, but it seems to us to be a rather graceless way to express oneself. We prefer to use a few extra words, if necessary, to say what we mean. Rather than "Anyone caught with drugs is subject to a fine and/or imprisonment," we would write, "Anyone caught with drugs is subject to a fine or imprisonment or both." Even better: "Anyone caught with drugs may be fined or imprisoned or both." Often, either conjunction is by itself sufficient to express the thought.

The slash (/), or virgule, is not a standard punctuation mark and perhaps should be used only in legal or technical documents, where we concede it serves a useful purpose.

aren't I? (never)
Let's say you stretch your body and yawn, "I'm rather tired, aren't I?"

Aren't I? As in "Are I not?" Oh, oh. That's a singular pronoun *(I)* yoked to a plural verb *(are)*.

English seems to have a special attraction for contractions—*isn't, aren't, they're, he's, we'd,* and the like—so it seems strange that there is none for *am not*. Logically, *am not* would be contracted as *amn't,* but the process of linguistic evolution, which is rarely logical, has rejected that. *Ain't* has been around more than two centuries, but, like comedian Rodney Dangerfield, it don't get no respect. It is, in fact, generally considered to be an illiteracy.

The lack of a contraction for *am not* causes no particular problem until we need to use the phrase as a question. A simple statement such as "I am not invited to the party" can be expressed both naturally and correctly as "I'm not invited to the party." But "Ain't I invited?" is nonstandard, and "Am I not invited?" sounds affected or stuffy to some ears.

Many speakers and writers, especially in Britain, have settled on *aren't I* as a solution to the dilemma. To our ears, *aren't I*? is at least as affected as *am I not*?, and the latter has the advantage of being both logical and consistent with traditional grammatical form. For our part, we'll go with *am I not*? and leave *aren't I*? to our British friends.

We think *amn't* would make a good and useful addition to our language. When we're elected national language co-czars, we'll see to it.

at this [particular] point [in time] (never)
The airline flight attendant drones, "At this time, we are making our initial descent into O'Hare." The presidential press secretary tells reporters, "At this particular point in time, the president has not made a decision on that."

At this time, at this particular time, at this point, at this point in time, at this particular point in time, at the present time, and *at present* all mean the same thing—*now*. In fact, the verbs that usually accompany those fatuous expressions have *now* "built in." In the first example, *are* means "are now"; in the second, *has not* means "has not now," so all the other words add not a scintilla of meaning.

Unless there is a need for *now* as emphasis, the verb is sufficient.

average person (sparingly)
Everyone knows that Yogi is smarter than the average bear, but who knows how to measure a bear's intelligence? *Average,* properly, is a mathematical concept, so *average person* (or bear) is an imprecise locution. Although *average person* is readily understood and widely accepted, we suggest *typical* as a much better adjective.

basically (sparingly)
If you mean "at the root of it all," as in "She is basically a good person," feel free to employ this adverb. But most people use *basically* as a verifying adverb, as in "Basically, we missed the bus." Basically, you know what we mean.

comprised of (never)
To the careful writer, the expression *comprised of* is gibberish. *Comprise* means "include." Thus, *comprised of* makes no more sense than *included of*.

The whole comprises the parts: "The alphabet comprises twenty-six letters." *Compose* means "make up." The parts compose the whole: "Twenty-six letters compose (make up) the alphabet," or, in the passive voice, "The alphabet is composed of twenty-six letters." Whenever you want to use *comprise,* ask yourself whether *include* would work. If so, you're okay; if not, choose a synonym. Whenever you're tempted to say or write *comprised of,* resist.

consensus of opinion (never)

Consensus of opinion is a common member of the Department of Redundancy Department. *Consensus* means "agreement," so *of opinion* is a useless appendage. *General consensus* is also redundant. *Consensus* is all you need. *Consensus* is sometimes misspelled "concensus," probably out of a false association with *census*. If you associate *consensus* with *sense,* you will have no trouble spelling the word correctly. *Consensus,* incidentally, is not necessarily unanimous agreement.

could care less (never)

This illogical and clearly incorrect expression is a corruption of the cliché *couldn't care less,* which means that one cares not at all so caring less would be impossible. *Could care less,* if it means anything, means that one cares, because otherwise it would be impossible to care less. Only careless writers and speakers use it.

In our opinion, the language would not be poorer without either of these overused expressions.

criteria is (never)

A famous paraphrase of a line from Virgil's *Aeneid* is "Beware of Greeks bearing gifts," but Greeks, or rather the Greek language, have given some good and useful words to English. One of these is *criterion,* a standard for measurement. Many people will live to a ripe old age never knowing there is such a word, but almost everyone knows the word *criteria,* which is the plural of *criterion*. The problem is, there is a general impression that *criteria* is singular, and we often see or hear the word used in sentences like "The most important criteria for good writing is clarity." Remember: One criterion plus one criterion equals two criteria. One criterion; two or more criteria.

Another Greek-derived word, *phenomenon,* is troublesome in the same way though perhaps not to the same extent. *Phenomenon* is singular; *phenomena* is plural.

eke out (carefully)
The writer who uses *eke out* must be careful to use it correctly. Many writers do not. To *eke out* is to augment or supplement, as in "As a writer, I eke out my income by doing neurosurgery on weekends." It is wrong to use *eke out* to refer to a final result, as in "The Dow Jones Average today eked out a small gain." If you want to be certain you have used *eke out* correctly, try substituting *add to.* If that doesn't work, something is wrong.

Eke is never used alone. It is always followed by *out.*

enormity (carefully)
When something is very large, it is said to be enormous. The quality of being enormous is enormousness. Even though *enormousness* and *enormity* are linguistic cousins, they have different meanings. *Enormity* means "the state of being wicked, monstrous, outrageous." We can speak of the enormity of Stalin's crimes against the Russian people, but we should not use *enormity* to describe the size of the former Soviet Union. For that we need *enormousness.*

enthuse (sparingly)
Nouns with suffixes usually derive from verbs—*pronunciation* from *pronounce, demolition* from *demolish, abandonment* from *abandon,* and so on. *Enthuse* is what linguists call a back-formation because it is a shortened verb that comes from a noun—*enthusiasm.* Although the word is accepted by many scholars and good writers, it has not yet been accorded universal respectability. It's not a word we use, but we cannot in good conscience fault those who do. If you are enthusiastic about *enthuse,* fine; but be aware that many authorities consider it colloquial.

equally as (never)
In this sense, *equally* and *as* mean the same thing, so *equally as* is redundant. Use one or the other, not both.

everyday (carefully)
"I will always speak my mind. Every day," says a man in a Toyota TV commercial. The screen turns black, and the slogan materializes: TOYOTA/EVERYDAY.

The Toyota people goofed. *Every day,* styled as two words, is an adverb that means just what it says, as in "Every day in every way we get better and better." *Everyday,* squished together as one word, is an adjective meaning "commonplace, ordinary," as in "an everyday occurrence." Did the Toyota hucksters really want to say that their products are commonplace and ordinary? We don't think so.

When you mean "all days," write *every day,* not *everyday*.

famously (carefully)
In his 1998 book, *The Death of Outrage,* William J. Bennett writes, "James Madison famously wrote . . ." The former secretary of education, whose academic credentials are impressive, no doubt intended to say that Madison was famous for having written the statement attributed to him, or that the statement itself was famous.

Famously is an adverb. We learned in grammar school that an adverb modifies a verb, an adjective, or another adverb and tells when, where, or how. Mr. Bennett's sentence has neither an adjective nor another adverb, so *famously* must modify the verb *wrote*. But it does not tell when or where Madison wrote the statement. How about *how*? "James Madison 'in a famous manner' wrote . . ." makes no sense.

Famously used as Mr. Bennett uses it seems to be a recent visitor to our lexicon. Let us hope its visit is short.

feel badly (never)
Badly is an adverb. Used to modify the verb *feel,* it should tell how you go about the act of feeling. If you want to describe your physical condition, do not say or write, "I am feeling badly." Say or write, "I am feeling bad." If you are, let us say, a chiropractor whose job is to

feel your patient's spine to check the alignment of the vertebrae, you might say, "I am feeling badly today" to mean that you are not doing your job skillfully. If a hangover from last night's party is the cause of your ineptitude, you might say, "I am feeling badly today because I am feeling bad."

The same principle applies to *smell bad* and *smell badly*. If you smell bad, you need a stronger deodorant; if you smell badly, you need an olfactory nerve transplant.

I am feeling bad.

forego (carefully)
When the *Atlanta Constitution* reported that "leaders of both parties had urged Senate members to forego political grandstanding," that distinguished newspaper was really saying that the leaders had urged members to "go before" political grandstanding. The statement makes no sense.

Forego means "to go before." It is often confused with *forgo,* which means "to give up." The *Constitution* writer obviously meant *forgo. Forego* is rarely seen and in fact is hard to use correctly. Its present and past participles, *foregoing* and *foregone,* are common and are almost never misused.

If you write *forego,* be sure it means what you think it means. Chances are good that *forgo* is the word you need. Most of the time, you ought to forgo *forego.*

for free (never)
Free is an adjective, not the object of a preposition. We're not charging you extra for that information. We're giving it to you *for nothing;* we're giving it to you *free. Free* works best when it is free of adornment.

forté (never) **forte** (carefully)
Forte should neither be written with the stress mark on the *e* nor pronounced for-TAY. When the word is used to mean one's strong point ("Grammar is his forte"), the correct pronunciation is "fort," as in Fort Knox. *Forte* is also a musical direction meaning "loudly." When used that way, it is pronounced as a two-syllable word with the stress on the first syllable—FOR-tay.

Sad to say, many (perhaps most) people will assume that you are an ignoramus when you speak of your strong point as your "fort." If what people think of you is more important than the knowledge that you're right, you might want to stick with FOR-tay. But don't compound the error by saying for-TAY.

fortuitous (carefully)
Fortuitous is a perfectly good word, but it doesn't mean what a lot of folks think it means. It does not mean "lucky." It is not a synonym of *fortunate,* however much alike the two words look and sound. *Fortuitous* means "accidentally, by chance," as in "A fortuitous meeting of an old college friend led to Maria's being offered a job in the company." Of course, it was fortunate for Maria that she got the job,

but the sense of the sentence is that meeting her old friend was accidental, not planned.

from whence (never)
Ever-lovin' Adelaide, Nathan Detroit's ever-optimistic girlfriend in the wonderful old musical *Guys and Dolls,* sang "Take back your mink, from whence it came." Well, Miss Adelaide was not one of those "goils" who speak perfect English. If she had been, she would never have said "from whence." *From whence* is a common redundancy. *Whence* means "from what place" and should not be preceded by from.

Whence is a bit poetic for most uses, anyway. Few people would say, "Whence came she?" in ordinary speech or writing. Most would say, "Where did she come from?" And, yes, it *is* all right (but not alright) to end a sentence with a preposition, as you will see later.

fulsome (carefully)
"I do believe the time will come down the road," said former White House counsel Jack Quinn on NBC's *Meet the Press,* "when [President Clinton] will address these matters in a fulsome way. . . . [H]e will have another opportunity to more fulsomely discuss the matter."

Fulsome is not a synonym for *fully,* as Mr. Quinn evidently believes. Although we occasionally see the word used in a positive way, as in "the fulsome plant and animal life of the rain forest," the word most often has a strong negative connotation—"fulsome mounds of greasy food." Common synonyms include *overdone, beyond good taste, offensive, insincere,* and *repulsive.* Unless you are certain that the context will make the meaning unmistakable, you are advised to avoid *fulsome.* Never employ *fulsome* as a synonym for *fully.*

graduate college (never)
A public-service advertisement for a national organization that educates people about autism said, "Today, autistic people are graduat-

ing college, holding jobs . . ." Wrong! People who say that they "graduated college" need to return for a course in remedial English. A person may graduate *from* college or a college may graduate a person. Either is correct, but the latter is considered the more formal.

head honcho (never)

The word *honcho* was probably a linguistic stowaway on ships bringing American servicemen home from the Far East after the Korean War. It comes from the Japanese *hon cho,* a military squad leader. *Honcho* has evolved to mean a boss or leader of any kind. It's somewhat slangy and is fast becoming a cliché, but it's acceptable in informal speech and writing. *Head honcho* is redundant and should be shunned.

hone in (never)

Hone in appears in some newer dictionaries as an alternative to *home in,* as in "The missile will hone in on its target." Most writers, however, still consider *hone in* an error. We suggest that you avoid *hone in* and opt instead for the more traditional expression, *home in*.

hopefully (carefully)

We can just see the worms wriggling as we open this can. Edwin Newman, former TV superstar and author of several books on language, is said to have in his office a sign reading ABANDON HOPEFULLY ALL YE WHO ENTER HERE. The sign, if it exists, plays on the message engraved on the gate of Hell in Dante's *Inferno*. It illustrates the aversion that some experts feel for *hopefully* as it is most often used these days.

Used correctly, *hopefully* is an adverb that means "in a hopeful manner," as in "Mergatroyd approached his boss hopefully to ask for a raise." That means that Mergatroyd was full of hope when he approached his boss. No quarrel there from either Mr. Newman or us.

The problem arises when someone uses *hopefully* to mean "I hope," "one hopes," "it is hoped," or "let us hope," as in "Hopefully, the boss will give Mergatroyd a raise." In "Hopefully, the boss will give Mergatroyd a raise," *hopefully* cannot be an adverb because the sentence has no verb it can logically modify. The only verb is *will give,* and surely the intent of the sentence is not to say that the boss will give Mergatroyd the raise "in a hopeful manner." So, if *hopefully* is not an adverb in that sentence, what is it?

One problem with this construction is that many of your listeners or readers will ask themselves and you what *hopefully* modifies. Some would say that *hopefully* is a conjunctive adverb modifying the entire statement that follows. That interpretation raises a second problem. This vague usage fits absolutely with a modern tendency to displace responsibility—in this case a refusal to identify who is doing the hoping. Saying, "Hopefully, our school system will improve" is very different from saying, "I hope that our school system will improve." If you say, "I hope," the next question may well be "What are you going to do about it?"

Whenever you are tempted to begin a sentence with *hopefully,* back off and think about the meaning.

importantly (carefully)

Importantly is an adverb and should not be used except to modify a verb. In a sentence such as "More importantly, we completed the project on time," the only verb is *completed.* Because "importantly completed" is nonsensical, it is obvious there's no verb for *importantly* to modify. Grammatically, *more important* is elliptical for "what is more important." Thus, "What is more important, we completed the project on time." Some writers, even experienced ones, seem to love *importantly,* perhaps because they imagine it sounds, well, more important.

"The senator spoke importantly on the subject" is an example of the correct use of *importantly*. Use the word that way if you use it at all.

infer (carefully)

Infer is one of the most commonly misused words in English, and it would be sad if this constant misuse resulted in loss of meaning for such a useful word. To infer is "to draw a conclusion from what one sees or hears."

"The reporter inferred from the president's statement that he would not seek reelection" does not mean that the president actually said he would not seek reelection. It means that the reporter drew that conclusion from the statement.

The misuse of *infer* most often occurs in a sentence such as "The president inferred in his speech that he would not seek reelection." The correct word is *implied*. Remember this: The person speaking does not infer; he implies. The person listening does not imply; she infers.

irregardless (never)

"The incident and others like it told across the city . . . have a common theme—that irregardless of the benefit to children . . . his own political miscalculations . . . have greatly contributed to his present difficulties." That sentence, which we have mercifully condensed from fifty-four words, appeared in the vaunted pages of the *New York Times*—yet it contains the word *irregardless*.

Irrespective of what you have heard, *irregardless* is actually a word, and it's been around since at least the beginning of the twentieth century. But *irregardless* is a redundant blend of *irrespective* and *regardless*, and the result is a nonstandard double negative. *Regardless* is the correct word.

Caveat scriptor (writer beware): Of all the misuses that slither through the English language, *irregardless* will get you in the hottest of water.

kudo (never)

Don't let the *s* fool you: *kudos* is singular. It means "praise or approval." There is no such word as *kudo*. And be sure to pronounce that long *o* in *kudos*. A radio announcer always spoke of giving *kudus* to people who had done something praiseworthy. Whatever such a person would do with a "large, grayish brown African antelope with large, annulated, spirally twisted horns" is beyond us.

liable (carefully)
Which of the following sentences is correct?

> **If you commit a crime, you are likely to go to jail.**
> **If you commit a crime, you are liable to go to jail.**

Both are correct. Does this mean that *likely* and *liable* are synonymous? No. The two sentences have subtly different meanings. The first means that if you commit a crime, the chances are good that you will go to jail. The second means that if you commit a crime, you expose yourself to possible incarceration.

Liable carries a definitely unpleasant connotation; *likely* expresses simple probability with nothing unpleasant implied. The error we are cautioning against is the use of *liable* to mean *likely*.

literally (sparingly and carefully)
Literally is one of those words that pepper the writing and speech of people who aren't especially fastidious about the words they choose. During between-deal chatter at a bridge party, a woman tells a story about some unusual behavior of her cat and concludes with, "That cat is literally human."

Really?

A CBS radio sportscaster averred that flu-ridden Michael Jordan was "literally dead on his feet" when he led the Bulls to a last-minute victory over the Utah Jazz.

Literally dead on his feet? Remarkable—and grisly.

If we can believe those who use *literally* without regard to its meaning, people all over this great nation are dying of laughter, rolling in the aisles, climbing walls, breaking their neck to finish a job on time, and wading through mounds of cats and dogs after a rainstorm.

But *literally* means "actually," not "figuratively." Of course, the woman did not mean her cat was actually human. Nor do people literally die of laughter, roll in theater aisles, climb walls, or break their neck to finish a job. Even El Niño, the source of all bad weather in 1998, never afflicted Southern California with a storm that brought felines and canines falling out of the sky.

The use of *literally* in the manner described has been defended as a way to emphasize an obvious exaggeration. Even if one accepts that characterization, which we do not, the word most often appears in contexts that require no emphasis. Hyperbole and metaphor, useful devices in writing and speaking, ought to stand alone. If they're not apt enough to stand on their own, they're not worth using.

At best, *literally* is overused. We recommend that you employ *literally* literally—to mean "in a literal sense or manner." Your writing will be a lot better. Literally and literarily.

media is (never)

Media is plural and should not be used with a singular verb form. It seems especially egregious, and certainly illogical, to write, "The news media *is* doing a good job of covering the Senate hearings, but *they* have not dug deeply into the subject." That's trying to have it both ways, making *media* both singular and plural in the same sentence.

When we use *news media* as singular, we seem to be implying (not inferring) that the news media of the nation are combined into a giant, monolithic entity. That concept is simply untrue. It is an example of how fuzzy thought can produce fuzzy writing—and vice versa.

We acknowledge that we're swimming against the tide on this one, but we maintain that correct usage is *media are,* whether we are speaking of news media or artists' media. Now repeat after us, *media* is plural, *media* is plural, *media* is plural. . . .

millennium (carefully)

Near the end of the 1990s, the word *millennium* began to appear often in the news media and elsewhere. No problem with that, except that many people, including some who ought to know better, insist that January 1, 2000, marks the first day of the "new millennium." Not so. The new millennium begins on January 1, 2001. A millennium is a thousand years; therefore the last year of a millennium must end in zero. The same logic applies to century. The last day of the nineteenth century was December 31, 1900; the first day of the twentieth century was January 1, 1901.

Millennium is often spelled wrong—"milennium," "millenium," or even "milenium." *Millennium* derives from two Latin words, *mille,* "thousand," and *annus,* "year"—thus, two *l*'s and two *n*'s.

miniscule (never)

The correct word is *minuscule,* which is an adjective meaning very small. "Miniscule" is more than a misspelling. It is a nonword that is slithering into the language and making a fair bid to supplant *minuscule* or at least to gain respectability as a "variant."

We suspect that "miniscule" gained currency when the "mini-" craze (*miniskirt, minicourse,* and the like) hit the language in the mid-1960s. And, if "miniscule" comes, can "maxiscule" be far behind? *Yuk! Aaargh! Bleeeeah!*

The opposite of *minuscule* is *majuscule,* which isn't seen often.

myself (sparingly)

Pronouns that end in *self* or *selves* (*myself, yourself, himself, herself, themselves,* etc.) are called reflexive pronouns. We often hear (and sometimes read) *myself* and other *-self* pronouns when simple personal pronouns would not only suffice but would seem less pretentious than a *-self* pronoun. Examples: "The Joneses invited my wife and myself to the dinner party"; "Fine, and yourself?" (in answer to "How are you?").

Why do people use reflexive pronouns in those ways? We believe there are two reasons: (1) To avoid using *I* or *me*, which some people mistakenly think sounds egotistical, and (2) to give their discourse a touch of what they imagine to be elegance. Neither of these has any legitimacy.

We can think of three legitimate uses of a reflexive pronoun:

1. As the object of a verb when the subject and object are the same person: "Tom Dooley held himself erect until just before they slipped the noose over his head." In that sentence, using *him* rather than *himself* would create an ambiguous statement, because Tom could have been holding someone else erect.
2. As an intensifier: "She, herself, baked the cherry pie for Billy Boy" or "She baked the cherry pie herself." In these sentences, *herself* could be omitted, but the sentences would be weaker.
3. In such idiomatic expressions as "all by myself," "me, myself, and I," and "Help yourself to another serving of *frijoles negros*."

nauseous (never)
One of the many anomalies of our language is that a word can have two meanings that seem to conflict with each other. These are called contronymns, and one or the other meaning usually disappears sooner or later. Such is the case with *nauseous*. Traditionally, *nauseous* is an adjective meaning "disgusting." Thus, if you say, "I feel nauseous," you may be conveying an unfavorable impression of yourself to a listener who accepts the traditional meaning of *nauseous*.

A second meaning of *nauseous* is "afflicted with nausea." This meaning seems to be gaining ground and is, according to the *Merriam-Webster's Collegiate Dictionary*, used more often than the first. Although we would like for the traditional meaning to be preserved, we are realistic enough to understand that when change is inevitable, the best course is to relax and watch it happen. The traditional meaning of *nauseous* is the one that seems likely to fade away. Therefore, we recommend, with some regret, that you do not use *nauseous* at all. If you want to say "afflicted with nausea," use *nauseated.* If you want to describe something or someone as disgusting, try *nauseating, sickening, revolting,* or *repulsive.*

off of (never)
Off stands alone nicely. *Of* is a useless appendage.

one of the only (never)
This strange and illogical expression began showing up a few years ago, and English took a step backward when it did. The expression has been defended on the ground that it is no worse than *only two,* because *only* means "one" and *only two* is oxymoronic. A specious argument! It's like saying that robbing a bank is okay because it's no worse than robbing a jewelry store. Moreover, *only* in the sense of "only two" does not mean "one"; it means "no more than." There is no meaning of *only* that fits in *one of the only*. Do not say or write *one of the only*. Choose *one of the few.*

overexaggerate (never)
Overexaggerate is overkill. Spare your readers a fate worse than overdeath.

parameter (carefully)
Parameter is a term for the variable in a mathematical equation. It is often used incorrectly, especially in business writing, to mean limit, boundary, dimension, or even scope, as in "Let me describe the parameters of the problem." We suspect that this misuse stems from

parameter's similarity to *perimeter*, which is the outer boundary of a geometrical figure. We recommend that you leave *parameter* to mathematicians, engineers, and statisticians.

penultimate (carefully)
"Governor George W. Bush is the penultimate last resort," intoned CNN news anchor Bernard Shaw, "and I guess the Supreme Court is the next to last resort."

Mr. Shaw was referring to a convicted murderer's chances for a reprieve. If the U.S. Supreme Court refused to stay the execution, the last resort would be an appeal to Governor Bush for clemency. It's hard to say what Mr. Shaw meant. We can only guess that he did not know the meaning of *penultimate*.

Whenever you see or hear *penultimate*, the odds are good that you are seeing or hearing a word misused. That's because the correct use of *penultimate*, which means "next to last," as in "1999 is the penultimate year of the twentieth century," is relatively rare. Most people who use the word believe it means something like the best, or the last word, as in "Rolls-Royce is the penultimate luxury automobile." *Ultimate*, which means last, does connote superiority; *penultimate* does not.

per your request (never)
This expression, common in business correspondence, ought to be consigned to the linguistic dustbin. At best, it is too stiff for modern style.

person that (never)
Although *that* as a relative pronoun referring to a person has a long history in English—e.g., "One of those still plain men that do the world's rough work." (Lowell, "On Grant's Bust")—most modern stylists use *who* when referring to a person and *that* when referring to a thing. We recommend that you do likewise.

pour over (carefully)
If you are pouring over this book, we hope the pages dry so someone else can pore over it. *Pore over* means to study carefully or gaze at intently; *pour over* means, well, nothing unless you insert an object for the transitive verb *pour,* as in "pour the gravy over the turkey."

reason is because (never)
Reason is because is a redundancy. Use *reason is that.* . . . The reason we recommend "reason is that" is that the grammatical subject, *reason,* is balanced by a noun clause in the predicate, headed by *that.*

reverend (carefully)
Properly, *reverend* is an adjective applied to the name of a person to be revered, usually a member of the clergy. It is not, however, a title comparable to *Mister* or *Doctor*. Thus, it is incorrect to address a minister as "Reverend Jackson." The correct use is "the Rev. Jesse Jackson" or "the Reverend Mr. Jackson."

Similarly, *honorable* is an adjective often used with the names of politicians, as in "the Honorable Trent Lott." We doubt that anyone would refer to Senator Lott as "Honorable Lott."

Having made our point, we acknowledge that *reverend* is commonly used as a title, even by the revered ones themselves, and that many educated people consider it acceptable. We are sticking to our guns on this one, however, and suggest that you eschew the use of *reverend* as a title.

successfully (carefully, sparingly)
Here's a challenge: Write a sentence using *successfully* without being redundant. It's easy. We just did. Naaah! that doesn't count.

Most of the time, the adverb *successfully*—and often the adjective *successful*—does create a redundancy. We recall reading about a man who "made his first successful parachute jump at the age of ninety."

One must wonder how many unsuccessful jumps the gentleman made before he became a nonagenarian.

there's (carefully)
"Here's hundreds of tax deduction ideas for home-based businesses and independent contractors!" advertises the NCRA Store. Increasingly, we are seeing and hearing contractions involving adverbs and singular verbs that are followed by plural nouns—"There's ten reasons to sharpen your writing skills." Make that "There are ten reasons to sharpen your writing skills." Use *there's* or *here's* only with a singular subject—"There's a place I love to visit."

those kind (never)
The use of *those* (or *these*) *kind* is another error that pervades the speech and, on occasion, the writing of even educated people. *Those* and *these* are plural and should modify plural nouns. The correct expression is *that* (or *this*) *kind* or *those* (or *these*) *kinds*.

try and (never)
"Try and take your club back a little more to the inside," the golf pro tells the duffer who has just sliced a ball into the next ZIP code.

The use of *try and* for *try to* is common in everyday speech and increasingly common in writing. *And* is a conjunction, but it is not used as a conjunction in the example. It does not join two actions, "try" and "take." Instead, it substitutes for *to* as the beginning of what should be an infinitive, *to take*. In grammatical terms, the infinitive functions as a noun, the object of the transitive verb *try*. (Try what? Try to take. . . .)

As far as we know, the practice of using *and* instead of *to* as an infinitive starter occurs only when the infinitive follows the verb *try*. We think it is slovenly in speech and indefensible in writing.

undoubtably (never)
There is no such word. *Undoubtedly* is correct.

unique (carefully and sparingly)
Unique is an overworked word that is often used incorrectly. Etymologically, *unique* is related to *unit, uniform, united,* and the like—all of which denote "oneness." Hence, if *unique* means "one," it must not be modified. Something cannot be more unique, less unique, very unique, or extremely unique. It is either unique (one of a kind) or not. We are suggesting "carefully" for *unique* to remind readers to use the word correctly and "sparingly" to remind them that *unique* has been so much overused that it has all but lost its effectiveness.

viable (carefully and sparingly)
An editorialist, discussing Dr. Kervorkian's grisly (no, not *grizzly*) calling, wrote, "When all hope of recovery is gone, suicide is a viable option."

Viable? Well, no. *Viable* means "capable of living." When physicians speak of "a viable fetus," they make sense. When businesspeople say that closing a plant is a viable option, they're using a word as it was never meant to be used. Yet business literature is replete with viable options, alternatives, plans, programs, products, and actions—and even chairmen of the board.

Fad words come and go, but for our part they come too fast and go too slowly. Who knows when *viable* crawled out of the medical textbooks, wormed its way into the general vocabulary, and became a business fad word? It should have stayed where it belonged, where it served a useful purpose.

Whenever you're tempted to use *viable,* try *feasible, workable, doable, possible, sustainable, practical, practicable,* or another synonym—unless, of course, you mean "capable of living." By the way, if you do choose to use *viable,* remember that nothing can be more viable or less viable. It's either capable of living or not.

would of (never)

Would of is simply sloppy pronunciation of *would have,* but it shows up in print now and then. It shouldn't.

x-times less (never)

The *New Yorker* magazine quoted anthropologist Helen Fisher as saying that female chimpanzees "are twenty times less likely to bicker over rank." Leaving aside the intriguing question of how an anthropologist can determine the likelihood that chimps will bicker over anything, we must question how one can use times (which denotes multiplication) and come up with something less.

This is not an uncommon error. We have seen it written by good writers and published in good publications. The correct rendition of the point would be that males are twenty times more likely to bicker over rank.

y'all is (never)

With the election of Jimmy Carter as president, Southern speech suddenly became chic. Books were written on how to "speak Southern," but that didn't keep non-Southerners from butchering the colorful regional dialect. For example, many could never accept the fact that *y'all* (*you all*) is plural. No respectable Southerner would say, "John, what are y'all doing here all by yourself?"

A poem by that famous Irish writer Anne O'Nymous (Anonymous) clarifies the plurality of the one-syllable *y'all:*

> Y'all gather 'round from far and near,
> Both city folk and rural,
> And listen while I tell you this:
> The pronoun "y'all" is plural.

If I should utter, "Y'all come down,
Or we-all shall be lonely,"
I mean at least a couple folks,
And not one person only.

If I should say to Hiram Jones,
"I think that y'all are lazy,"
Or "Will y'all let me use y'all's knife?"
He'd think that I was crazy.

Don't think I mean to criticize
Or that I'm full of gall,
But when we speak of one alone,
We all say "you," not "y'all."

We note that *you all*—but not *y'all* (at least not yet)—is used increasingly by Americans other than Southerners as the second-person plural pronoun rather than simply *you*, which can confuse because of its dual-purpose nature as either singular and plural.

you know (sparingly)

The vacuous expression *you know* has been spreading (in speech, though not, thank heaven, in writing) like the most virulent cancer for decades. Edwin Newman, in his book *Strictly Speaking* (1975), noted, "The prevalence of *y'know* is one of the most far-reaching and depressing developments of our time, disfiguring conversation wherever you go." And Senator Robert Byrd, of West Virginia, entered into the *Congressional Record* (May 8, 1991) a tirade titled "The Inane Expression 'You know.' "

But it was left to Barney Oldfield, an eighty-seven-year-old retired air force colonel, to launch a vigorous campaign against *you know*. In 1997 Colonel Oldfield, a Nebraskan, offered a $1,000 scholarship to the Nebraska student who submitted a tape recording of a radio or television broadcast with the most *you knows* in fifteen minutes.

The first year's winner was thirteen-year-old Dalton Hartman, who submitted a tape with forty-one *you knows* in four minutes, thirty-eight seconds. The next year, a fifth grader named Jason Rich took the prize. His tape, a twelve-minute interview with a basketball coach, had sixty-four *you knows*. Here, with the names changed to protect the negligent, is a brief excerpt transcribed from the tape:

> *You know,* Joe has been [unintelligible]. We started him in the second half when Harold was in foul trouble and I have just been really pleased, *you know,* with his progress, *you know*. He had a real tough assignment there, *you know,* of guarding Jones, *you know*. I don't know if that's a good match or not, *you know,* but he's growing more comfortable with that type of play. . . . I think him [sic] and Dan don't get enough credit. I think they're both really good and they can do things for us both defensively and offensively and Dan gets fifteen rebounds tonight, *you know* what I mean, and he was just a warrior around the boards. He also has four assists, *you know*. Joe comes in and the thing that Joe brings to the table, and we've been working with him . . . but *you know*. I thought Bobby Smith came in and played extremely hard, *you know*. He couldn't come up with a break, *you know*—couple of baskets—but he's getting closer and closer and . . .

And so it goes, on and on. If the excerpt seems a bit surreal, just listen for *you knows* the next time you turn on your radio.

Colonel Oldfield has made arrangement in his estate for continuation of the contest. Bless you, Colonel; may your tribe increase.

III

Lightning Bugs and Lightning

One night not long ago, your *Sleeping Dogs* authors simultaneously dreamed that they picked up the morning newspaper and read the following item:

> PODUNK, USA—Two men, one of whom is believed to be a two-thousand-year-old Roman army officer, are

being sought in connection with last week's murder of a large brown bear, Podunk Police said today. The two men fled the murder scene by hitching a ride on the back of a young sheep. Police Chief Joe Schmoe has predicted the men will soon be caught and has urged them to join the police force. "It will go easier on them if they do," he said.

Several prominent citizens have criticized the police for their inability thus far to enroll the fugitives in a local musical group. Chief Schmoe asked that these concerned citizens emulate their family physician.

"Just take off all your clothes and join us for a while," he said. "You can be sure these criminals will get nothing but ice cream and cake."

Believe it or not, this article really appeared. Well, not exactly. It's a composite, cobbled from examples of word abuse and misuse we have encountered not once but many times in the nation's press. If you don't quite "get it," try this version:

PODUNK, USA—Two men, one of whom is believed to be a hundred years old, are being sought in connection with last week's grisly murder, Podunk police said today. The two men fled the murder scene and are still on the lam. Police Chief Joe Schmoe has predicted the men will soon be caught and has urged them to turn themselves in to police. "It will go easier on them if they do," he said.

Several prominent citizens have criticized the police for their inability to corral the fugitives. Chief Schmoe asked that these concerned citizens have patience.

"Just bear with us for a while," he said. "You can be sure these criminals will get their just deserts."

We have read countless reports of "grizzly" *[grisly]* murders. We don't recall one committed by a centenarian (a hundred-year-old person), but we have seen articles about centurions (Roman officers) observing their hundredth birthday. More times than we can count, we've read items about someone "turning himself into a police officer." Of course, fugitives are often "on the lamb *[lam]*."

O.K. Chorale

Horses are put in chorales.

In the world of the press, people other than doctors are urged to have patients *[patience]*, horses are put in chorales *[corrals]*, and men and women of impeccable reputation are often asked to bare *[bear]* with someone. Many a miscreant has been given his "just desserts" *[deserts]*, no doubt to the chagrin of those who wanted the guy to be punished.

Examples of atrocious usage abound, not only in the press but elsewhere in this great but linguistically challenged land of ours. Lest you think we exaggerate, we offer a handful of examples from our bulging files:

- From the *Grand Rapids Press*, Grand Rapids, Michigan: "When World War II broke out two years later, her father and brother were interred *[interned]* in camps in the U.S."

• From a publication of the American Academy of Pediatrics: "The chapter committees meet at the desecration *[discretion]* of the committee chairman."

• From the *Northern Star,* student newspaper of Northern Illinois University: "He said it is something different than *[from]* the monogamy *[monotony]* of dining every day in the residence halls." (Well, we suppose monogamy is monotonous to some people.)

• From *North Coast Bowler,* Brook Park, Illinois: "Three Ladies Indicted *[inducted]* Into Hall of Fame."

• From a letter from the director of Chicago's Court Theatre: "[The play is] taught *[taut],* funny, and prodigiously smart." (We are impelled to comment that if a play is taught, it must be smart.)

• From the *Times-Record,* Brunswick, Maine: "The Depression taught me to horde *[hoard].*"

• From *Bear Prints,* a newsletter of Washington University: "Former Saint Louis U. Coach Joe Clarke Handed Men's Soccer Coaching Reigns *[reins].*" (Bad usage reigns at Washington U.)

• From the *Arizona Republic,* Phoenix: "A substantial contingency *[contingent]* . . . would prefer that the city remain true to its charter."

• From the *Concord Monitor,* New Hampshire: "[Ronald] Reagan said he was eager to return to the state where he began his duel *[dual]* careers in film and politics." (We suppose Mr. Reagan fought many a duel in the political arena.)

• From a parking lot sign at Genentech Corp.: "Only vehicles with Genentech stickers or placards are aloud *[allowed]* beyond this point." (Keep those car horns quiet, folks.)

• From the *Argonaut,* student newspaper of the University of Idaho: "[Comets] are made up of organic material, ice and miscellaneous gases and are thought to be ruminants *[remnants]* from the beginning of the universe." (Comets and ruminants have at least one thing in common: Both have tails.)

• In a college library: "No bear *[bare]* feet allowed."

• From the newsletter of the Sierra Club in Crestline, California: "This extraordinary lady . . . was one of those rare humans who becomes [sic] a legion *[legend]* in her time."

• From an ad for an alcoholism treatment method, published in the *Orlando Sentinel:* "[The method] allows the person to be a social drinker and control the addition *[addiction]*.

• From *Imprimis,* a publication of Hillsdale College, Michigan: "As Shakespeare wrote, 'Sweet are the uses of diversity *[adversity]*.' " (This is taking political correctness too far!)

• From the *Atlanta Constitution:* "Manager Bobby Cox showed off a recent addition to his office, a huge laminated menagerie *[montage]* of clippings from last year's championship series." (Wait until the animal-rights crowd hears about this.)

• From an Associated Press dispatch: "About 125 people turned out under cloudy skies Saturday, including 15 ancestors *[descendants]* of Victorio's Warm Springs Apaches." (A ghostly gathering, no doubt.)

• From the *San Antonio Express News* (headline): "Cellular services near omniscient *[omnipresent]*." (Those cellular phones are a bunch of know-it-alls.)

• From the *San Jose Business Journal:* "During the last decade, the direction of Wolverine World seemed to hang in libido *[limbo]*." (If one must hang, hanging in libido might not be all that bad.)

What has caused this erosion of our ability to use the right words? Television, for one thing. By and large, we have become a nation of viewers and listeners rather than readers and thinkers. In the age of TV, precision takes a backseat to impression. Image becomes everything. When it comes to word abuse, high-priced television personalities are among the worst abusers.

Another problem is overreliance on computer spell checkers, which are a marvelous technology when used properly but are no substitute for knowing what a word means and how to spell it. No spell checker can distinguish between homophones—*rein/reign, horde/hoard, loan/lone,* for example.

But differences and precise meanings are important to anyone who wants to write or speak well. Mark Twain said it best: "The difference between the almost right word and the right word is really a large matter—'tis the difference between the lightning-bug and the lightning."

From the perspective of having spent many years as writers, editors, teachers, and—most important—readers, we have determined that the ten most common word confusions are, in approximate order of frequency: *lie/lay, fewer/less, different from/different than, amount/number, compose/comprise, farther/further, disinterested/uninterested, affect/effect, imply/infer,* and *among/between.*

To help you separate the lightning from lightning bugs, we offer below a glossary of often abused, confused, and misused words and phrases. We have designed this chapter as a quick-reference guide, not a substitute for a good dictionary or comprehensive usage manual. We have made no attempt to discuss all definitions and possible nuances of each word; rather, we focus on the areas where confusion most often reigns (not *reins*).

ability, capacity *Ability* and *capacity* may be used interchangeably in some contexts, but in others there is a subtle distinction to be made. *Ability* connotes accomplishment; *capacity* connotes "the right stuff." It could be correct to say that a person has the capacity to be a fine musician even lacking the ability to play "Chopsticks" on the piano. In other words, ability comes from making use of capacity. The fuel tank of your automobile might have a capacity of twenty gallons, but until you drive into a service station and fill 'er up, the capacity means nothing.

accident, incident An accident is an unforeseen or unplanned event, something that occurs by chance: an automobile accident, a chance meeting. An incident is an occurrence of minor importance and brief duration.

adverse, averse In a *Concord* (New Hampshire) *Monitor* story about a new mall, a local businesswoman called the mall authorities to seek space to set up shop: "They said they were not adverse to giving local people first chance."

That caused an *adverse* (read "unfavorable") reaction from your *Dogs* authors. *Averse,* an adjective always followed by *to,* means "to be opposed to." We are averse to the confusion between *adverse* and *averse*.

adopt, adapt, adept Both *adopt* and *adapt* are verbs. To adopt is to take something as your own. To adapt something is to change it: "The company adopted a new approach to the problem and adapted its organizational structure accordingly"; "Margaret adopted Sue's recipe, but she adapted it for her taste."

Adept is an adjective meaning proficient: "This book will help you become adept at writing clearly and correctly."

At one time the Japanese were said to follow the practice of adopting the technology of other nations, adapting it for their own purposes, and becoming more adept at it than its originator. Today, however, the Japanese are adept at developing their own.

advise, inform *Advise* means to give counsel; *inform* means to give information. One should not write "Please keep me advised of your plans."

affect, effect What word pair comes up as a question most often to word watchers? *Affect/effect.* To *affect* something is to exert influence on it; to *effect* something is to make it happen. *Effect* as a noun is a result or an outcome. By far the most common occurrences are *affect* as a verb and *effect* as a noun. When something affects you, it has an effect upon you.

affluent, effluent These two words have a common ancestor, but their meanings are very different. *Affluent* is an adjective meaning prosperous; *effluent* is a noun referring to something that flows out, such as a stream. Most often, it refers to wastes discharged from a manufacturing plant or a sewage-treatment facility. Examples: "Americans today are more affluent than ever"; "The river was polluted by effluent from a nearby chemical plant."

aggravate, irritate To *aggravate* something is to make it worse; to *irritate* is to create a new condition: "He was irritated by not having received the check, and the fact that it was for the wrong amount aggravated the situation."

Exacerbate is a synonym for *aggravate; annoy* is a synonym for *irritate*.

alter, altar *Alter* is a verb meaning "to change." An altar is a structure, a mound, or a platform where ceremonies, such as weddings, take place. After you have been led to the altar, your life is altered forever.

alternate, alternative *Alternate* can be used as a noun to mean one who is empowered to act for another, such as a convention delegate. Usually, however, it is an adjective or a verb. It is not interchangeable with *alternative,* which is a noun that implies a choice. Strictly speaking, the choice should be between two possibilities, but most writers today use *alternative* when the choice is among several. *Alternative* should not be used as an adjective, as in *alternative choice.*

alumnus, alumna, alumnae, alumni If a man said, "My wife is an *alumnus* of Princeton," the Latin scholars among us would give him a strange look. That's because *alumnus* is a masculine word. The feminine word is *alumna* (pronounced a-LUM-nuh). The plural of *alumnus* is *alumni* (pronounced a-LUM-nigh; the plural of *alumna* is *alumnae* (pronounced a-LUM-ni, with the *i* being short, as in *little*). *Alumni* can also refer to either men or women and is always used for both when both are parts of a compound subject.

If this all sounds confusing, these examples should make everything clear:

Helen is an *alumna* of Northwestern.

Helen and Marjorie are *alumnae* [or *alumni*] of Northwestern.

Paul is an *alumnus* of Northwestern.

Paul and Bruce are *alumni* of Northwestern.

Paul, Bruce, and Helen are *alumni* of Northwestern.

The pronunciations we have given are correct in modern English, even though they differ slightly from the pronunciations Julius Caesar probably used.

amount, number "A normal heart beats about 3.5 billion times in a lifetime. We're working to expand that amount," reads an ad for Mount Sinai Hospital. Mount Sinai's motto is "Take Good Care of Yourself." We agree. But we ask the Samaritans at Mount Sinai to take good care of their sentences. The last word in the statement should be *number*, not *amount*.

The distinction between these words is similar to the distinction between *few* and *less* (qv). *Amount* is used for bulk quantities; *number* is used for countable quantities. Thus, a large number of dollars makes a large amount of money.

anxious, eager The primary meaning of *anxious* is "worried"; it is an unpleasant sensation. *Eager* means "enthusiastic, desirous" and denotes pleasant feelings. We are eager to finish writing this book, but we're anxious about whether anyone will read it. Thanks, by the way, for relieving our anxiety.

apparent, evident The difference between *apparent* and *evident* is apparently slight, but it's worth knowing. "The man apparently had been drinking" would be appropriate if the man was seen staggering. "The man evidently had been drinking" would be appropriate if some tangible evidence was found, such as empty beer cans on the car seat beside him. Sometimes one or the other of those words is used when some other word would express the thought more precisely. For example, if the evidence was especially strong, "It was obvious that the man had been drinking" would be better.

apprise, appraise To *apprise* means to inform; to *appraise* means to evaluate. Do not write "Keep me appraised of your progress."

assume, presume The distinction between these two words is becoming blurred. Their meanings are indeed close, but there is a subtle difference that ought to be preserved. To *assume* is to take for granted without any evidence. To *presume* is to believe something to be true, but with reason or logic. Stanley used *presume* correctly when he met Livingston and said, "Dr. Livingston, I presume."

assure, ensure, insure To *assure* is to promise (someone); to *ensure* is to make certain; to *insure* is to safeguard. Bergen and Cornelia Evans, in *A Dictionary of Contemporary American Usage,* offer an excellent illustration of how these words differ: "To be well insured ensures peace of mind and is vastly assuring."

average, mean, median, medium *Average, mean,* and *median* are often confused. *Average* is determined by adding a series of quantities and dividing by the number of quantities. Thus, the average of 10, 25, 100, 80, and 70 is 57 (285 divided by 5).

Mean is the halfway point between two extremes. If the high temperature for the month was 74 and the low was 36, the mean temperature of the month was 55. To calculate the mean, subtract the lower number from the higher, divide by 2, then add the result to the lower. (74 minus 36 equals 38; 38 divided by 2 equals 19; 19 plus 36 equals 55—the mean).

Median is the tricky one, the one some people assume is the same as *average*. The median is the middle number in a series of quantities. Stated another way, half the numbers are above the median and half are below. In the seven-quantity series of 10, 37, 43, 60, 150, 161, and 250, the median is 60. If the series has an even number of quantities, add the two middle numbers and divide by two. In the eight-number series of 2, 4, 7, 10, 18, 30, 46, and 110, the median is 14. (10 + 18= 28, divided by 2 equals 14).

No educated person should confuse *median* and *medium,* but some do.

awhile, a while *Awhile* is an adverb meaning "for a while," as in "Let's stop awhile." *Awhile* should not be used as the object of the preposition *for* or *in.*

bi-, semi- These prefixes are often confused, and logic is of little help in keeping them straight. *Bi-* means "two," *semi-* means "half." Thus, a bimonthly publication is printed every two months; a semimonthly is printed twice a month. *Biannual,* however, means "twice a year," as does *semiannual. Biennial* means "every two years."

bilateral, multilateral We occasionally read a reference to a "bilateral agreement" that involves more than two agreeing entities. *Bilateral* ("two-sided") should not apply in such a reference. An agreement involving more than two would be *multilateral* ("many-sided"). *Trilateral,* of course, means three-sided, but *multilateral* is acceptable for an agreement that involves three entities. *Unilateral* (one-sided) usually implies that one party is acting alone.

bring, take *Bring* implies motion toward the speaker or writer; *take* implies motion away from the speaker or writer. Thus, we bring in the newspaper, but we take out the trash. Well, sometimes.

burglar, robber The acts committed by these two disreputable characters are different. Burglary is breaking and entering, usually with intent to commit a crime such as theft. Robbery is the taking of property directly from a person by force or threat of force. A careful writer would not write of robbing a house, because a house is not a person.

can, may *Can* denotes the ability to do something; *may* denotes permission. Most of us learned that in grammar school when we asked the teacher, "Can I be excused?" and she answered, "No, you may not until recess." Somehow, we held on.

capitol, capital A *capitol* is a building in which a legislature meets. A *capital* is the city in which the capitol is located. *Capital city* and *capitol building* are redundancies. *Capital* also refers to money.

career, careen *Career* most often refers to one's job, but it can also mean to travel straight ahead at a high rate of speed, as in this headline in the Johnstown (Pennsylvania) *Tribune-Democrat:* CAREERING CAR'S CRASH COULD HAVE BEEN WORSE.

We, your dedicated grammar guys, are delighted—and, to be honest, astonished—that the headline writer got it right. *Career* as a verb seems almost to have disappeared. In fact, many readers assume it to be a typographical error when someone uses it correctly. Indeed, the woman who showed us the headline above thought she was presenting us with an error. But the derivations are clear: The often misused *careen* issues from the Latin *carina,* "a ship's keel," and means to sway from side to side. *Career* comes from the French *carriere,* "a racehorse."

cement, concrete Concrete is what sidewalks are made of. Cement is a powdery ingredient of concrete. In the interest of precision, do not refer to a concrete wall as "a cement wall."

cheap, inexpensive The difference here is one of connotation. *Inexpensive* hints of good sense; *cheap* connotes shoddiness. No one wants to wear cheap clothes, but most of us do not mind inexpensive ones. Do not write "cheap price."

compare to, compare with Use *compare to* when discussing things that are dissimilar. Use *compare with* when discussing things of the same category. A company's profits for one year may be compared *with* its profits for the previous year, but a lively child should be compared *to* a young colt.

compliment, complement Because these words sound alike, they cannot be misused in speaking. They are, however, misused often in writing. *Compliment,* as a noun or a verb, is an expression of praise. To *complement* is "to supplement or complete." A good mnemonic device is to visualize *complement* as *comple(te)ment.*

concept, idea When we first thought about writing this book, it was merely an idea. But an idea was not enough to persuade St. Martin's Press to offer us a book contract. For that we needed a concept. Turning the idea into a concept involved developing an outline and writing some sample copy.

Concept is much overused, especially by writers who want to make something seem more important or more advanced that it is.

consensus *Consensus* means agreement, but not necessarily unanimous agreement. The word often appears in the redundant *consensus of opinion* and is sometimes misspelled "concensus." Writers can avoid this misspelling by remembering that *consensus* implies a *sense* of the subject among those who have agreed.

consistent, constant *Consistent* means "regularly occurring"; *constant* means "unending" (figuratively or literally):

She consistently hits drives straight down the fairway.
She plays golf constantly.

consist in, consist of In his excellent treatise, *Economics in One Lesson,* Henry Hazlitt wrote, "The art of economics consists in looking not merely at the immediate but at the longer effect of any act or policy." Perhaps a less careful writer would have written "consists of" in that context.

Consist of introduces a discussion of components: "An infantry battalion consists of three companies." *Consist in* introduces a definition or a discussion of identifying characteristics, as in Hazlitt's sentence. *Consist in* is rarely misused; *consist of* often is.

contagious, infectious All else being equal, an infectious disease is much more troublesome than a contagious disease. At least it's more difficult to contain. To contract a contagious disease, you must come in contact with a carrier or something (such as a drinking glass) that the carrier has used. An infectious disease spreads on its own, through the air or another medium.

continuous, continual *Continuous* means "unbroken"; *continual* means "repetitive." This distinction is not always easy to make, but these examples will help:

The Great Wall of China runs continuously for 1,500 miles.

The telephone rang continually after we won the Publishers Clearing House Sweepstakes.

controversial, contentious When used to describe a person, *controversial* means that different people view the person differently. A contentious person, on the other hand, is one who is quarrelsome.

convince, persuade These words are often used interchangeably, but the distinction between them is worth preserving. To *convince* someone is to bring that person to your point of view. To *persuade* someone is to induce that person to do something. For example, if you are convinced that this is a useful book, you may be persuaded to buy it. Remember that *persuade* is usually followed by an infinitive, but *convince* never is.

credit All the various definitions and connotations of *credit* are favorable, and except for its use in accounting, the word has no good antonym. Perhaps this is why we often hear *credit* used in situations where an antonym would serve better. For example, "The player was credited with four strikeouts in the game." Credited? Not likely, unless the player was attempting to throw the game and the gamblers were giving him his due.

democracy, republic When we pledge allegiance to the flag of the United States of America, we pledge allegiance "to the republic for which it stands." Why not the democracy for which it stands? Technically at least, the United States is a republic, not a democracy. In a democracy, the people make decisions by direct vote, as they do in California and other states when initiatives are on the ballot. In a republic, the people elect representatives who, for better or worse, act on their behalf.

On the other hand, Winston Churchill, who knew a thing or two about both government and language, wrote a book called *The Great Democracies,* so it is difficult for us to get exercised when we hear our country called a democracy. Still, we prefer *republic* and recommend it.

deny, refute One can deny what is said about oneself, but if one wants to refute the accusation, one must offer proof.

deprecate, depreciate To *deprecate* is "to disparage, disapprove of, belittle, make light of." To *depreciate* is "to lower the price or value of."

die of, die from Careful writers write that a person *died of,* not *died from,* a disease. The person written about is dead either way, but good usage lives!

discomfort, discomfit At first glance, these two related words might seem to be the same. They are not. *Discomfort* can be either a noun or a verb. As a noun, *discomfort* is the state of being uncomfortable. As a verb, it means to make uncomfortable. *Discomfit,* which is always a verb, means "to defeat, thwart, foil, embarrass, disconcert, perplex, or puzzle." The state of being discomfited is discomfiture.

discrete, discreet These homophonic adjectives are quite different in meaning. *Discrete* means "separate"; *discreet* means "prudent." Although *discreet* and *discrete* share a Latin ancestor and are pronounced identically, they have discrete meanings that are observed by discreet users of language.

disinterested, uninterested *Disinterested* means "impartial"; *uninterested* means "unconcerned." A trial judge should be disinterested but not uninterested. An uninterested judge might be bored and might prefer to be at home watching reruns of *Perry Mason*.

dissociate, disassociate Both words mean "to separate from," but *dissociate* has been around longer and is preferable. The additional syllable in *disassociate* adds weight but not strength. Both take the preposition *from*.

distinguish, differentiate To *distinguish* is to perceive differences; to *differentiate* is to point out differences:

> The man's eyesight was so poor that he was unable to distinguish the sky from the water.
>
> Scientists are able to differentiate among dozens of different species.

distrust, mistrust The difference between *distrust* and *mistrust* is one of degree. *Distrust* implies solid ground or strong evidence. *Mistrust* is a vague or undefined uneasiness. One might distrust an accountant who has had problems with the IRS or mistrust a pilot because of an innate fear of flying. Both *distrust* and *mistrust* can be a noun as well as a verb.

dominating, domineering These words are closely related but have vastly different connotations. *Dominating* means "occupying a position of power, influence, or preeminence." *Domineering* connotes bullying:

> The Yankees were the dominating force in baseball for many years.
>
> She was the victim of a domineering husband.

effete, effeminate *Effete* means "used up, marked by weakness or decadence." *Effeminate* means "having feminine qualities not typical of a man."

egotist, egoist It is obvious that both these words come from the Latin *ego,* meaning *I,* but the difference between them escapes many people. Most are aware that an egotist is one who thinks and talks mostly about himself. An egoist, though, is one who believes that self-interest is the motive for everything and the valid end for all action. Unlike an egotist, an egoist might be quite modest and not at all inclined to talk about herself.

emigrate, immigrate The choice depends on whether the subject is coming or going. One emigrates from one country and immigrates to another. A person who emigrates is an emigrant or émigré (pronounced EM-uh-gray); a person who immigrates is an immigrant.

eminent, imminent *Eminent* means "prominent, noteworthy, outstanding, celebrated, illustrious, distinguished." *Imminent* means "near or impending":

Stephen Hawking is perhaps the most eminent physicist of our time.
In 1941, America's entry into the war seemed imminent.

In law, the power of the government to appropriate private property for a public purpose is called eminent domain. If the government abuses that power, destruction of our freedom may be imminent.

etc., et al., i.e., e.g. These four Latin abbreviations are similar and often confused. *Etc.,* the most familiar, stands for *et cetera.* It means, simply, "and so on" or, literally, "and the rest." It is used for things only, not people. *Et al.* stands for *et alii, et aliae,* or *et alia,* depending on whether it refers to masculine, feminine, or neuter. It means, literally, "and others" (men, women, or things). The abbreviation is the same for all three.

In speech the full Latin phrase, *et cetera,* is pronounced. *Et al.* is properly expressed as "and other [men, women, or things]" or simply as "and others." Note the period after *al.*

I.e. stands for *id est* and means "that is." It introduces a clarification of what precedes it. *E.g.* stands for *exempli gratia* and means, literally, "for the sake of example." The most common misuse is *i.e.* for *e.g.* A good memory jogger is to think of *e.g.* as standing for "example given." Your high school Latin teacher might not have approved, but it works.

feasible, possible An undertaking may be possible, but it might not be feasible if the cost seems too high.

ferment, foment *Lonely Planet* magazine, November 1996, contained this sentence: "Solomon's heavy taxes fermented discontent among his people." Although *ferment* means "to agitate to cause a state of intense activity," the word is best used to describe the chemical process that converts sugar to alcohol. *Foment* means "to stir up or set in motion events that could change the status quo." *Fomented* would be better in the example.

fever, temperature Everyone has a temperature all the time, but only a sick person has a fever.

few, less Use *few* (or *fewer*) for things that are counted, *less* for things that are measured in other ways. Thus, fewer dollars, less money; fewer hogs, less pork; less food, fewer calories; less hay, fewer bales.

flaunt, flout "The Government of Iran must realize," said President Jimmy Carter to the United Nations in asking the U.N. to approve sanctions, "that it cannot flaunt with impunity the expressed will and law of the world community."

President Carter didn't mean to flaunt his word abuse in front of the world, but he did make a mistake. *Flaunt* means "to show off, usually ostentatiously;" *flout* means "to ignore contemptuously." Rich people may flaunt their wealth, and bons vivants their knowledge of fine wines. Reckless drivers flout the traffic laws—and Iran, in this case, flouted "the expressed will and law of the world community." Indeed, it is almost always the law that gets flouted.

flotsam, jetsam These two nautical terms often appear together. When they do, they are not redundant. Flotsam is the floating wreckage of a ship or its cargo after a shipwreck; jetsam is stores, equipment, or other materials thrown overboard (jettisoned) during an emergency to lighten the load.

foreboding, forbidding A foreboding (noun) is a feeling or sense that something evil or ominous is about to happen. *Forbidding* (adjective) means "grim, difficult, dangerous, menacing":

> She looked with foreboding on the forbidding task of climbing Mount Everest.

foreword, forward A foreword is a brief comment at the beginning of a book. *Forward* describes movement toward a point in time or space.

founder, flounder *Founder* means "to sink or to fall." It is used most often to refer to a ship, but it can refer to a building, an animal, or even a person. *Flounder* means "to struggle or to thrash about in disarray."

> The ship foundered during a storm.
>
> Witnesses said the man floundered in the water for several minutes before disappearing.

Flounder can provide good imagery when used figuratively:

The company floundered for nearly two years before it declared bankruptcy.

Sometimes a company flounders and then founders. A flounder is also a flat fish that's delicious broiled.

further, farther Use *farther* for distance, *further* for time or for a continuation of something other than distance. The choice is not always clear-cut, but most good writers make the distinction most of the time.

gourmet, gourmand A gourmet is a connoisseur of food, a person who appreciates culinary delicacies. A gourmand is a step removed from a glutton, who is also excessively fond of eating but is not as particular about what he or she eats. *Gourmet* is a complimentary term; *gourmand* usually is not.

hanged, hung The old admonition "pictures are hung, people are hanged" is still valid.

healthy, healthful Increasingly we see *healthy* used to describe proper diet, exercise, relaxation, and other healthful habits. But *healthy* is more appropriately used to describe a person or animal who is in good health. To describe something that promotes good health, choose *healthful.*

historic, historical The distinction here is fine but worth making. *Historic* should be reserved for places, things, and events of great significance:

The Old North Church is one of the nation's most popular historic attractions.

President Reagan's nomination of Sandra Day O'Connor to the Supreme Court was an event of historic importance.

The Magna Carta is perhaps the world's most precious historic document.

Historical refers to history, often in the sense of a particular period of history, or to history as a subject:

Artifacts from the Civil War are of historical significance, but they have little monetary value.

Use the article *a* rather than *an* with both *historic* and *historical*.

in behalf of, on behalf of To speak *in behalf of* someone is to plead that person's case. To speak *on behalf of* someone is to speak in the person's stead. A lawyer may speak both in behalf of and on behalf of a client.

incredible, incredulous Something that is incredible is unbelievable. People who do not believe are incredulous. *Incredulous,* which can apply only to a person, is the more often misused.

invent, discover A panel on boxes of Cheerios cereal illustrated "great discoveries"—the roller coaster, the skateboard, the yo-yo, and the jigsaw puzzle. Discoveries? Well, no. Inventions. Alexander Graham Bell didn't discover the telephone; he invented it. The Curies didn't invent radium; they discovered it.

irony, sarcasm Irony and sarcasm often involve similar expressions, but sarcasm is meant to wound someone. If you say, "Great shot!" to a golf opponent who has just plopped a tee shot into the lake, that's sarcasm. If you say it to yourself after you've done the same thing, that's irony.

its, it's Because the apostrophe is used to form the possessive of nouns, many writers carelessly use *it's* as the possessive of *it,* as in "The leopard doesn't change it's [its] spots." Of course, possessive pronouns (*his, hers, mine, ours, its,* et al.) exist on their own and are not "formed" by apostrophes. You will do well to remember that the apostrophe can also indicate a contraction, which it does in the case of *it's.*

In summary: *Its* is the possessive form of *it*; *it's* is the contraction of *it is.*

lectern, podium Discriminating speakers and writers use *podium* (from the Greek *podia,* "the foot") to mean the small base on which a speaker stands and *lectern* (from the Latin *lectura,* "to read") for the slant-top desk on which the speaker places notes. This distinction seems well on its way to being lost, with *podium* becoming the all-purpose term for the base, the stand, and the entire stage.

like, such as Writers whom we respect disagree on whether there is any significant difference between *like* and *such as.* Wilson Follett and Theodore Bernstein say no. James J. Kilpatrick says yes. We come down gingerly on the side of Kilpatrick. His argument seems valid: "When we are talking of large, indefinite fields of similarity, *like* properly may be used. . . . When we are talking about specifically named persons [places or things] . . . included in a small field, we ought to use *such as.*" In "Books like this one can help you write better," *like* means similar to. In "Cities such as Atlanta and Birmingham are important to the economy of the Southeast," the intent is to specify those cities as examples, not merely to put them into a broad category of cities that are important to the economy of the Southeast.

loan, lend Traditionalists, especially in Britain, who insist that *loan* is a noun and cannot be a verb have lost that particular battle. *Loan* and *lend* are interchangeable as verbs, except in a few idiomatic expressions. Antony could never have exhorted the Roman crowd to "loan me your ears."

loathe, loath What a difference a little *e* makes. *To loathe* is to feel intense dislike or even hatred. *Loath* is an adjective meaning "reluctant." Discerning listeners and readers loathe hearing or seeing *loathe* used to mean *loath.*

majority, plurality A majority is any amount more than 50 percent. A plurality is the highest of three or more numbers when none is a majority. If a candidate wins an election with 40 percent of the votes cast, the candidate has won with a plurality of 40 percent.

may, might There is little difference between *may* and *might* when they're used to express uncertainty. Most of the time the two are interchangeable. To the sensitive ear, however, *might* connotes a slightly greater degree of uncertainty:

> If you read this book, you may learn to write better and you might even earn more money.

In speech, *might* would be emphasized slightly to show greater doubt. Technical differences in *may* and *might* relate to tense, but they are not troublesome enough to discuss here.

minimize, diminish To minimize is to reduce something as much as possible; to diminish is to reduce something by an indefinite or unspecified amount. Good law enforcement can diminish crime, but one would be hard pressed to say that crime has been minimized, no matter how much it has been diminished.

mitigate, militate *Mitigate* comes from a Latin word meaning "to soften," and that meaning is pretty much intact in modern English. To *mitigate* is "to lessen the effect of some circumstance or event":

> The judge allowed the man's good driving record to mitigate the sentence.

Militate, which also came from Latin (*militare,* to engage in warfare), means "to oppose, or work against." *Militate* is almost always followed by *against:*

> The man's poor work record militated against his getting the job.

mobile, movable Promoters of the mobile-homes industry like to say that most mobile homes stay put. No doubt that's true. But it is also true that mobile homes can be moved. That makes them movable. *Mobile,* on the other hand, describes something (or someone) that can move (as opposed to can *be* moved). A person may be immobilized by an injury, even though a doctor may determine that the person is movable. In that sense, *movable* means that the victim can be moved without endangering life. *Immovable* usually refers to something in a fixed position—e.g., a tree, a mountain, or a large structure.

oral, verbal Almost everyone has read or heard the expression "a verbal agreement." Almost always that expression was employed to describe an agreement that someone didn't commit to writing.

Verbal, in other words, commonly serves as a synonym for *oral* and an antonym for *written*. But all language is verbal, as we can see from the Latin *verbum,* "word." Thus, speech is oral, writing is written, and both are verbal activities. Samuel Goldwyn seemed completely to confuse that point with his famous dictum: "A verbal contract isn't worth the paper it's written on."

We would prefer that *verbal* and *oral* be applied as they were intended to be used, but the use of *verbal* as a synonym for *spoken* is ingrained in the language.

Pablum, pabulum *Pabulum* (not capitalized) is a food that nourishes a plant or an animal. The word is also used figuratively to mean food for intellectual thought. *Pablum* (capitalized) is a trademark for a brand of baby food. Both words are used to describe something that is excessively simple or bland. Manufacturers usually cannot register a common word for use as a trademark, so they sometimes work a little creative magic on the spelling and come up with something they can protect. We wonder whether the Pablum folks created their trademark by misspelling *pabulum*.

persons, people Usually, you can trust your ear to tell you the right choice between *people* and *persons*. *People* is acceptable in virtually any context; *persons* is inappropriate for large numbers of people. In fact, with all numbers, *people* is preferable. "Six persons" comes across as stuffy.

precipitate, precipitous These two useful adjectives sound much alike and are often confused. *Precipitate* means "sudden, abrupt, rash, unwise." *Precipitous* means "very steep":

The horse made a precipitate dash down the precipitous hill.

prescribe, proscribe These two words are almost opposites. To *prescribe* is to lay down a rule or course to be followed. To *proscribe* is to prohibit as harmful or unlawful. If your physician prescribes a medicine, you had better take it. If the good doctor proscribes exercise, you had better be a couch potato.

preventive, preventative Although *preventative* is acceptable, *preventive* is much the better choice for both the noun and the adjective.

principle, principal *Principle* is always a noun. It means "a fundamental," as in "This book sets forth some of the principles of good usage." *Principal* can be either a noun or an adjective. As an adjective, it means "main" or "most important":

> The principal ingredients of salad dressing are oil and vinegar.

As a noun *principal* can refer to a person who is the administrative head of a school, to a partner in a business, to a party in a legal agreement, or to a sum of money:

> Our principal is a person of high principles who will not sacrifice his principles to add to his principal.

Despite the existence of a well-known memory jogger, these two words are often confused. Most elementary school students learn that the princi**PAL** is their pal. They also learn to think of the word as princip**A**l, letting the big *A* stand for "adjective." This tells them that *principal* is either a person or an adjective.

proceed, precede *Proceed* means "to go forward" (*pro-* means "forward"); *precede* means "to go before" (*pre-* means "before"). Because *procedure* is derived from *proceed,* it is sometimes misspelled "proceedure."

prone, supine After the tragic mass suicide in San Diego in the spring of 1997, a police spokesman was quoted in the press as saying, "They were all laying [sic] on their backs in a prone position. . . ." Wrong! If the victims were on their backs, they were not prone.

Prone means "facedown." The officer should have quit while he was behind and left it at "lying [not *laying,* though] on their backs," but if that wasn't good enough, he could have used *supine,* which means "face up." Mnemonically, when you are supine, you lie on your spine.

raise, raze These words have the same pronunciation but are almost opposite in meaning. *Raise* means "to lift up"; *raze* means "to tear down."

reticent, reluctant *Reticent* means "uncommunicative, unwilling to speak, reserved, taciturn." *Reluctant* means "hesitant, unwilling, averse." Although both words connote unwillingness, *reticent* usually refers only to speech.

seasonal, seasonable When referring to a season of the year, choose *seasonal. Seasonable* means "timely, opportune." "Seasonable weather" is accepted as idiomatic, but not "seasonable fruits and vegetables."

sewage, sewerage Sewage is waste; sewerage is the system of pipes that carry the sewage to wherever sewage is carried, not, let us hope, into our rivers and streams. *Sewerage* should not be used as an adjective. To do so is to be redundant. In "The developer installed sewerage lines in the subdivision," "sewerage lines" is redundant. "Sewage lines" would be acceptable in that sentence, but *sewerage* is the better choice.

site, cite These soundalikes are unrelated. *Site* is usually a noun meaning "location," as "the site of a building." *Cite* means "to call attention to."

The engineer chose an excellent site for the building.
The teacher cited three examples of good writing.

Site is used sometimes as a verb meaning "to place on location":

The engineer sited the building well.
The building was well sited.

In the latter example, *sited* is a better choice than *situated.*

stalactite, stalagmite If you're a spelunker, you probably know that a stalactite is a deposit of calcium carbonate that hangs from the "ceiling" of a cave and a stalagmite is a deposit of calcium carbonate that sticks up from the "floor." A good way to keep them apart is to let the *c* in *stalactite* stand for "ceiling." Forget the one about "stuck tight." Something can be stuck tightly to the floor as easily as to the roof.

stanch, staunch *To stanch* is to stop something, as in "stanch the flow of blood." *Staunch* means "loyal or steadfast," as in "staunch supporter."

stimulant, stimulus A stimulant produces a short-term effect; a stimulus is longer lasting. Coffee is a stimulant that temporarily increases some bodily functions. A tax cut is a stimulus to business.

tandem, parallel People often use *in tandem* when they mean *parallel.* Rails on a train track are parallel, but the cars of the train are in tandem.

this, that As demonstratives, *this* and *that* are used interchangeably by many writers. They should not be. *This* refers to something close at hand, such as this book that I am holding and this idea that I am discussing. *That* refers to something more remote in distance or time: that book on the shelf, that idea we discussed yesterday.

transpire, occur Some dictionaries now list *transpire* as a synonym for *occur*. Many authorities, however, consider it loose usage. The traditional meaning of *transpire* is "to leak out (as a vapor) and thus become apparent." Used that way, *transpire* strongly connotes the airing of information previously secret:

It finally transpired that the grand jury was investigating the agency.

The battle to preserve this traditional and useful meaning is probably lost, but we still would not use *transpire* to mean *occur*. There are better synonyms for *occur*, such as *happen, take place*.

trusty, trustee Although both *trusty* and *trustee* refer to people who are trusted, their connotations are vastly different. A trusty is a prisoner whose good behavior has earned certain privileges not given to other prisoners. A trustee is a member of the governing body of an institution or, in law, one who holds "in trust" the property of another.

Novelist John Grisham, in his bestseller *The Chamber,* refers to a convict whom prison officials have given special privileges as a "trustee." A trusty might be flattered to be called a trustee, but it seems likely that a trustee of, say, Harvard would take umbrage at being called a trusty.

turgid, turbid *Turgid* means "swollen"; *turbid* means "cloudy or muddy":

The child's belly was turgid from malnutrition.

The old man's eyes were turbid as a result of cataracts.

* * *

In his hilarious essay on the literary offenses of James Fenimore Cooper, Mark Twain laid down eighteen rules that govern the literary art. This was his Rule 13: “Use the right word, not its second cousin.” Home (not *hone*) in on the right word—the one that, in Twain’s unerringly right words, “lights the reader’s way and makes it plain.”

In writing at least, avoid lightning bugs and second cousins.

IV

Things You *Know* That Just Ain't So

The fact that you are reading this book leads us to conclude that you sincerely want to write and speak correctly and are looking for some guiding principles that will help you do so. You're not alone. We often hear from people who want to know the "rule" that governs some grammatical construction. For example, a letter from an attorney asked whether it is permissible to "split" a main verb from its auxiliary, as in "McPfoofnick has consistently been late for work."

"I know," the attorney wrote, "that it is incorrect to split an infinitive, but I'm not certain if the rule applies to verbs."

Incorrect to split an infinitive? Tell that to John Donne, Samuel Pepys, Daniel Defoe, Robert Burns, Samuel Taylor Coleridge, George Eliot, Arthur Conan Doyle, Rudyard Kipling, Abraham Lincoln, Henry James, and a host of others who have been promiscuously splitting infinitives since the 1300s.

The attorney's query illustrates one of the misconceptions—or myths, if you prefer—that we encounter in discussions of language. We call these misconceptions "Things you *know* that just ain't so." Like the attorney, who *knows* it is incorrect to split an infinitive, you may be laboring under one or more strongly held beliefs that have little or no validity in contemporary English. If so, reading this section could relieve you of some anxiety.

We have identified ten of the most enduring grammatical misconceptions and have presented them below in what might well be the order of the tenacity with which they are held.

Myth no. 1: It's wrong to ever split an infinitive.

An infinitive is a verb preceded by *to—to eat, to destroy, to understand.* A split infinitive is an infinitive in which *to* is separated from the verb by one or more words—*to hungrily eat, to willfully destroy, to thoroughly understand.*

There is little support for the notion that placing one word or more between *to* and the verb in an infinitive is a grammatical error. That notion began rearing its harmless head when early grammarians tried to force English to follow the same grammatical rules as Latin. In Latin and in the romance languages it sired, the *to* is "built in" and cannot be separated from the verb. That's because romance language infinitives are single words, like *hablar* in Spanish, which means "to speak."

Splitting the infinitive is sometimes necessary to convey the meaning you intend. For example, in "He decided to promptly return the money he found," *promptly* clearly relates to *return*. Moving *promptly* to another location in the sentence eliminates the split infinitive but changes the meaning. "He promptly decided to return the money he found" tells the reader that the finder *decided* promptly, but it says nothing about how long the finder planned to keep the money before returning it. Placing *promptly* immediately before the infinitive could leave the reader uncertain whether the word applied to *decided* or *return*. Placing it immediately after the infinitive makes it clear that *promptly* relates to *return,* but the construction seems awkward. Putting *promptly* at the end of the sentence is out of the question because it then would seem to modify *found*.

In some instances, avoiding a split infinitive is almost impossible, as in "The chairman said he expects the company's net income to more than double this year." In that sentence, *more than* can go no other place. Interestingly, substituting *almost* for *more than* creates a less difficult problem. In "The chairman said he expects the company's net income almost to double this year," "almost to double" makes sense, but "to almost double" is the more natural word order.

Consider this headline from the *Atlanta Journal:* SENATE FINANCE PANEL VOTES HEAVILY TO NEARLY DOUBLE CIGARETTE TAXES. A headline writer laboring under the no-split myth might have written "Senate finance panel votes heavily nearly to double cigarette taxes," which is both dissonant ("heavily nearly") and confusing. (What, exactly, did the panel vote to do?) "To nearly double" is clearly required.

All this notwithstanding, we advise you to beware and be wary of interposing a number of qualifying words between *to* and its verb in an infinitive. "The company plans to immediately, and with as little fanfare as possible, remove the product from the market" is not incorrect, but "The company plans to remove the product from the market immediately and with as little fanfare as possible" is preferred.

To paraphrase the most famous split infinitive in our pop culture, you are allowed to boldly go where many, many men and women have gone before. Our advice is, don't hesitate to split an infinitive when doing so will make your meaning unmistakable or prevent an awkward construction. Otherwise, resist the temptation to split infinitives. If the practice bothers some readers (and dulls your grammatical Ginsu knives), why not eliminate as many splits from your writing as you can?

Myth no. 2: Never use a preposition to end a sentence with. Like the imagined rule against splitting infinitives, the notion that it is somehow wrong to end a sentence (or a clause) with a preposition likely grew out of early grammarians' attempt to force English to follow the rules of Latin. Nevertheless, the "rule" is unsupported by most modern grammarians and has been ignored by some of the finest writers of English prose, past and present. Henry W. Fowler, the grammarian's grammarian, settles the issue best: "Those who lay down the universal principle that final prepositions are inelegant are unconsciously trying to deprive the English language of a valuable idiomatic resource, which has been used freely by all our greatest writers except those whose instinct for English idiom has been overpowered by notions of correctness derived from Latin standards."

Have a look at this sentence from an article in the *New Yorker*, a well-edited magazine: "Ethel Waters had a light, lissome voice that she could do anything with—growls, falsetto, mimicry, improvisation, parlando." The sentence is smooth and natural. It would be less so as "Ethel Waters had a light, lissome voice with which she could do anything. . . ."

The most widely circulated anecdote on the subject has Winston Churchill scolding an editor who had presumed to correct a Churchillian sentence that ended with a preposition. Wrote the great man to the editor, "This is the kind of impertinence up with which I will not put."

The admonition against ending a sentence with a preposition is a relatively recent one. It may stem from the word itself: *Preposition* means place before (pre-position), which gives the myth a certain credibility. But as the Evanses point out in *A Dictionary of Contemporary American Usage,* "[T]o argue from this that a preposition must be placed before its object is like saying that a butterfly must be a fly."

Now that we have made the case that no writer or speaker should feel guilty for having ended a sentence with a preposition, let us concede the fact that placing a preposition after its object can result in a clumsy locution. Have you heard about the boy who has just gone to bed when his mother brings into his bedroom a book about Australia? Asks the child: "What did you bring that book that I wanted to be read to out of from about Down Under up for?"

Worth remembering also is that the end of a sentence is the point of greatest emphasis. "Wasting" that position on a relatively insignificant part of speech might weaken the sentence.

In summary: Place the preposition after its object, even at the end of a sentence or clause, if doing so results in a more natural, rhythmic sentence or adds to the meaning or impression you want to convey. Otherwise, place it before the object.

In either case, it's not something to worry about. Note that we didn't write "about which to worry."

Myth no. 3: And don't begin a sentence with a conjunction.

A conjunction is a word that joins two grammatically equivalent elements—words, phrases, clauses, and—yes—sentences. The most common conjunctions—*and, but, or,* and *nor*—are called coordinating conjunctions. Literature, going back to the tenth century, is replete with examples of sentences that begin with coordinating conjunctions. The first chapter of Genesis in the Old Testament contains dozens: "And God made the beasts of the earth according to their kinds and the cattle according to their kinds, and everything that creeps upon the ground according to its kind. And God saw that it was good."

We cannot, of course, look to the Bible as a model for writing today. We can, however, look to well-edited publications and well-respected writers. This sentence was written by the distinguished editor Norman Cousins and published in *Saturday Review:* "But let us suppose that somehow people would get where they're supposed to go."

When a conjunction begins a sentence, is it still a conjunction? Yes. What does it join? It joins its sentence with the previous one. And the sentence could just as easily be part of the previous one, in which case there would be two independent clauses. The difference is merely a matter of punctuation—a period instead of a comma or semicolon.

Beginning sentences with *and, but, or,* or *nor* is a valued rhetorical device in the style quiver of most writers, and it can be effective if not overdone. For example, compare the sentence you have just read with this: "Beginning sentences with *and, but, nor,* or *or* is a valued rhetorical device in the style quiver of most writers. And it can be effective if not overdone." To our ears, the two-sentence version is better. The two thoughts are joined by *and,* but the pause between the thoughts is dramatically stronger with the period than it would be with a comma.

The trend in modern prose is toward shorter sentences. And the use of two sentences, the second beginning with *and,* follows that trend.

Now consider a third version: "Beginning sentences with *and, but, nor,* or *or* is a valued rhetorical device in the style quiver of most writers. It can be effective if not overdone." Here we have a two-sentence version without the conjunction. The dramatic connection between the thoughts is lost when *and* is eliminated as the starter of the second sentence.

Which of the three versions is best? That's for you to decide. The purpose of this discussion is simply to put to rest the myth that beginning a sentence with a conjunction is always wrong. Now you can decide for yourself.

Myth no. 4: *Between* is never used with more than two entities.

If you were taught that *between* must always be used with two persons or things and *among* with more than two, you were taught well. Or were you? Well, yes and no. It is indeed true that you ought to follow that rule most of the time. Most? Why not all the time?

The "notion" of two is embodied, etymologically, in the *-tween* part of *between,* but the *between*-only-for-two rule is too simplistic to be taken as gospel.

Although *among* is never used with only two entities, *between* may be used with three or more entities to emphasize the separateness or individuality of each. For example, "The Department of Commerce oversees business activity between the states."

In "An agreement between Roosevelt, Churchill, and Stalin resulted in the division of Germany after World War II," *between* is preferred if not required. On the other hand, *among* is required in "A discussion among Roosevelt, Churchill, and Stalin resulted in the division of Germany after World War II" because the intent of the sentence is not to say that Roosevelt spoke with Churchill, then with Stalin; that Stalin had a discussion with Roosevelt, then with Churchill; and so on.

Here are some other examples in which *between* is clearly required with more than two entities:

Between 50,000 and 60,000 Americans die in traffic accidents each year.
Georgia is between Alabama, South Carolina, Florida, and North Carolina.
The choice was between Carol, Gertrude, and Joan.

If your ear does not tell you which is correct, your best bet is *between,* regardless of the number of entities.

If Shakespeare had chosen *Like You Like It* . . .

Myth no. 5: *Like* cannot be used as a conjunction.

If Bill Shakespeare had chosen *Like You Like It* instead of *As You Like It* as the title of his great comedy, he would have been right in harmony with those among us who can't always decide when to use *like* and when to use *as.* The main point of contention is whether it is appropriate to use *like* as a conjunction, which is to say when *like* is to be followed by a clause, as in "Why don't you love me like you used to do?"

Indecision on the subject is understandable when we consider the distressing lack of consensus among grammarians, writers, editors, and other authorities. Wilson Follett *(Modern American Usage)* tells us that "there is no point in discussing *like* as a conjunction, because in workmanlike modern writing there is no such conjunction." On the other hand, Bergen Evans (*A Dictionary of Contemporary American Usage)* says that those who consider it wrong to use *like* as a conjunction are in a minority. He names such distinguished *literati* as Shakespeare, More, Kipling, Shaw, Coleridge, Shelley, Keats, and Maugham, who have done so in their writing. Ted Bernstein (*The Careful Writer)* avers that "there is no logical reason why *like* should not be used as a conjunction," but admits that grammarians and others who do object to such use "are a force in the language as it exists."

So. Where do Lederer and Dowis come down on the issue? Squarely in the middle. We accept *like* as a conjunction in most informal writing and speech—"Winston tastes good like a cigarette should," "I wish I could shimmy like my sister Kate"—but we prefer *as* in more formal uses, as you must have noted from reading this discussion thus far. A good writer will not use *like* habitually to replace *as, as if,* or *as though.*

We have no problem with using *like* before a noun in a prepositional phrase, as in "She speaks like an expert on the subject." This means "similarly to." Conversely, "She speaks as an expert on the subject" means that she *is* an expert and speaks with recognized authority.

Myth no. 6: An *if*-clause always means subjunctive.

James J. Kilpatrick, the author and syndicated columnist, is an excellent writer whose books on usage occupy places of honor on our bookshelves. But Mr. Kilpatrick, like most of us, now and then exhibits signs of the "*if*-is-always-subjunctive" malady. In one of his language columns, he wrote, "Back when I was growing up, the finest wine glasses were made of lead crystal. At the tap of a fingernail, they gave off a magical chime. *If the crystal were flawed, all you got was a clunk* [emphasis added]."

Although Mr. Kilpatrick's writing usually gives off a magical chime, the emphasized sentence falls with a clunk upon the sensitive ear.

The subjunctive mood, or mode, is used to express a condition that is untrue or impossible (*if I were you; if I were rich,* etc.). Grammarians call such situations "conditions contrary to fact." The fact that *if* and *were* seem to go together like bagels and lox leads some writers to routinely use *were,* rather than *was,* when they write a clause beginning with *if.* In Kilpatrick's sentence, *were* is incorrect because the sentence is simply past tense and not necessarily an expression of something that is false. It is not a condition contrary to fact. It you converted the statement to the present, you would have "If the crystal is flawed, all you will get is a clunk." If the crystal had been determined to be flawless, the subjunctive would be in order, and the sentence might read, "If the crystal were flawed [untrue condition], all you would get was a clunk."

A full explanation of the subjunctive would consume several pages of complicated technical discussion. Indeed, some uses of the subjunctive seem to be fading from the language. Our point here is this: Do not assume that an *if*-clause always introduces the subjunctive. Sometimes an *if*-clause contains fact.

Myth no. 7: *None* is always treated as singular.

Which of the following is correct?:

1. None of us is going to the party.
2. None of us are going to the party.

If you answered sentence (1), you are correct. If you answered sentence (2), you are correct. If you're one of the many people who maintain that *none* means "not one" and must always take a singular verb, consider this sentence: "The bricklayers completed none of the work." In that sentence, *none* clearly means "not any."

Indeed, in most occurrences, *none* is closer in meaning to "not any" than to "not one." That's why "None of the toys are working" sounds more natural than "None of the toys is working."

Thomas Jefferson, discussing how vacancies occur in public offices, wrote, "Those by death are few; by resignation, none [not any]." On the other hand, John Dryden wrote, "None but the brave deserves the fair." There is no shortage of examples of both usages in American and English literature.

The argument is often advanced that *none,* being zero, cannot be plural. But the logic works both ways: Can zero be singular? We could debate that question, but we won't. Let us say simply that you can strike this off your worry list. Consider *none* as singular when you want to emphasize a single entity in a group. Consider it plural when you want to emphasize more than one, as Jefferson did when he coupled the plural verb *are* with *none*.

Myth no. 8: No sentence fragments.

Just about any well-taught sixth grader will tell you that every sentence must have a subject and a verb and that writing in complete sentences is imperative. Just about any good writer, however, will tell you that it's permissible to ignore that dictum now and then.

What we are talking about here is not the habitual, purposeless, unrestrained use of sentence fragments that we often see in advertising copy. We're talking about special effects—sentence parts used for dramatic impact.

In his powerful novel *Deliverance,* James Dickey wrote, "Ah, he's going to turn into something, I thought. A lesson. A moral. A life principle. A Way." Dickey was a poet first, a novelist second. His ear for cadence led him to use fragments rather than a long sentence. Very effective.

An advertisement for Ponte Vedra Beach Resorts offers another example. Following seventy-five or so words of conventionally punctuated descriptive copy come these sentence fragments: "Two world-class resorts. One spectacular vacation experience." This device is effective because it emphasizes or complements points made in the main body of text. It also saves space, which is almost always at a premium in ads.

Not all ad writers use the device effectively. An ad for a bank in Arizona includes these: "Through the years there's always been something Bank One has held in common. A no-nonsense approach to doing our jobs, based on a pretty simple idea." We see no reason for the long nonsentence. Generally, the more words that are used in a fragment, the less effective it will be.

Sentence fragments, if not overused, can be an effective rhetorical device. They can add drama and interest, prevent overlong sentences, and make reading easier. Much easier.

Myth no. 9: Avoid clichés like the plague.

Think back. Did you say "Good morning" to your spouse or covivant today? Did the friend you met on the elevator say, "Have a nice day"? Did you write a letter and sign it "Sincerely yours"? Do you enjoy hearing the late Frank Sinatra's best-loved song, "My Way"? If you answered yes to any of these questions, you have acknowledged that clichés are virtually unavoidable and, for the most part, harmless. "Good morning," "Have a nice day," and "Sincerely yours," have been used since Day One (cliché), and the song that fans of "Old Blue Eyes" (cliché) love so contains more clichés than a dog has fleas (cliché).

"The spoken cliché," says Robert S. Lee, a Canadian communications consultant, "is a sort of oral shorthand without which serious inconvenience would afflict society." Lee's observation applies also to the written cliché, but to a lesser extent.

It is difficult, perhaps impossible, to produce a large volume of copy without on occasion falling back on a comfortable, familiar expression that many would condemn as a cliché. Even so fine a writer as author and columnist George Will can be forgiven for employing, in a single column, "private pork," "lightning speed," "stay the course," "take the heat," "fill the void," and "beat a pell-mell retreat"—all of which are slightly grizzled. In context Will's use of those expressions seems appropriate and not in any way objectionable.

Cliché is a French word meaning stereotype, a plate used in printing. It implies a repetitive process of creating. In a sense all words and phrases are clichés, because repetition is the process by which language changes and new words enter the language.

Let us be clear about the purpose of this discussion. We are not condoning the unremitting use of worn-out expressions that seem to substitute for thought. Good writers work hard to find fresh ways of saying things. We're simply saying that familiar phrases, used thoughtfully, correctly, and purposefully, may be more than permissible; they can be desirable.

Everyone is entitled to dress down in jeans and sneakers now and then; no one wants to wear evening clothes all the time.

Myth no. 10: The passive voice is never used by good writers.

Voice is a grammatical term that describes the relationship of a verb to its subject. When the subject is the doer of the action, the construction is said to be in the active voice. When the subject is the receiver, the construction is in the passive voice. An example serves better than a definition: "Mary bloodied John's nose" is active; "John's nose was bloodied by Mary" is passive. Either way, John is bloodied, bowed, and humiliated, but the impressions the two sentences give the reader are different.

The passive voice is weak, pretentious, fuzzy, and evasive, and it uses unnecessary words. So the myth that the passive voice should never be used by good writers is not really a myth. Right?

Wrong. Good writers use the passive when they need it to say what they want to say. Sometimes the passive voice is the better choice; other times it is the *only* choice. Consider this sentence and try to convert it from passive to active:

The criminal was arrested, tried, convicted, and sentenced to prison.

Because the different actions *(arrested, tried, convicted, sentenced)* were performed by different agents, expressing the thought in the active voice would require many more words and terminal tedium would set in.

It is true that much bad writing is passive, but that by no means says that the passive voice alone is what makes it bad. Overuse of the passive is often a symptom of a deeper problem.

We will discuss active vs. passive in our "Ten-Minute Writing Lesson," in Chapter X. For now, we offer half a dozen instances in which the passive may be preferable to the active:

1. When two or more actions and doers are involved, as illustrated above.
2. When the doer of the action is unknown, unspecified, or irrelevant:

The great pyramids were built thousands of years ago.

3. When the doer is significantly less important than what is done:

The meeting was concluded after two hours of heated debate.

4. When the writer, for whatever reason, wants to be obscure or evasive.
5. When the writer wants to convey a less forceful message or impression.

6. When the passive seems smoother, more natural, or more rhythmic.

Strengthen your understanding of the different effects you can get by using one voice or the other. Don't be a slave to the passive, as some writers are, but don't try to avoid it altogether.

V

Put Your Words in Order

With admirable restraint (if we do say so ourselves), we will resist the temptation to make a joke about sin tax. Nor will we advise you not to tell your mother you're living in syntax. Every writer lives in—or at least *with*—syntax, for better or worse.

For the purposes of this discussion, a definition: *Syntax is the orderly arrangement of sentence elements to create meaning.*

Sounds simple, and it is. Simple or not, your syntax will surely find you out if you don't give it the attention it deserves. As Wilson Follett wrote, "Prose is not necessarily good because it obeys the rules of syntax, but it is fairly certain to be bad if it ignores them." Faulty syntax might result in writing that is ambiguous, unclear, funny, or all three.

Much of the bad writing we see in the course of our work is caused by the writer's having committed one or more of a relatively few syntactical sins. This is sad, because although the study of syntax can be complicated, the syntactical principles one needs to know in order to write well are not. Most syntactical problems can be avoided by the simple device of reading your own prose—aloud if necessary—and listening with a sensitive ear.

The purpose of this section is to help you develop the aural sensitivity you must have to be aware of and avoid syntactical miscues. To do this we will give some examples and comment on each. First, let's consider a few principles that, when ignored, often cause bad syntax:

(1) *Modifiers—clauses, phrases, adjectives, and adverbs—should be positioned as closely as possible to whatever they modify.*

This sentence is from the *Atlanta Constitution:* "[Psychologist B. F.] Skinner, who is known primarily for his theories of human behavior, will discuss how behavior analysis has influenced the use of the computer in the classroom at 11 a.m." "At 11 a.m." modifies "will discuss"; it tells when Professor Skinner will hold his discussion. The writer chose to place it at the end of the sentence rather than next to the verb phrase, making it syntactically related to another verb, *influenced.* The result was a ludicrous sentence. One of our favorite student bloopers that misplaces a modifying phrase is "Abraham Lincoln wrote the Gettysburg Address while traveling from Washington to Gettysburg on the back of an envelope."

The more modifiers are allowed to wander, the greater the chance of their being associated with the wrong part of the sentence. Adjectives are usually placed before the nouns they modify. Adverbs may be placed either before or after, depending on what the writer wants to emphasize. "Walk slowly" and "slowly walk" mean the same thing but have somewhat different connotations. The writer must rely on the ear to know which is the better choice.

(2) *Sentence elements that are parallel in meaning should be of the same grammatical construction.*

"Reading, fishing, and to swim in the surf are the things I enjoy most at the seashore" is a sentence obviously weakened by unparallel elements. Even a writer with the tinnest of ears would know that the third activity is out of sync with the other two.

Although faulty parallelism can cause ambiguity, its victims most often are grace and style. Abraham Lincoln concluded his masterful Gettysburg Address, which he might have written on the back of an envelope but not while traveling on one, with "[T]hat government of the people, by the people, for the people, shall not perish from the earth." If, instead, he had proclaimed, "government of the people, conducted by the people themselves, and to the benefit of the entire population," the sentence elements would have lacked parallelism and power. It is unlikely his words would be quoted as often as they are.

(3) *When a pronoun is used, the noun to which it refers (its antecedent), whether expressed or understood, must be clear.*

This sentence appeared in *Newsweek:* "He [fugitive Eric Rudolph] left five $100 bills on Nordmann's table and disappeared in his 1977 Nissan pickup truck." Whose truck did Rudolph take? Nordmann's or his own? The antecedent of *his* is unclear, and the meaning of the sentence is in doubt. It would have been easy for the writer to clarify it by writing *Nordmann's* instead of *his*. Some writers dislike using a word or a name twice in the same sentence, but if that is a "sin," it is a far lesser sin than writing something that is unclear.

In a sentence such as "I read the book and liked it," the pronoun *it* clearly refers to *book*. But in "Please remove the dust jacket from the book and put it on the coffee table," the reader cannot be certain whether *it* refers to *book* or to *dust jacket*.

(4) *The relationship of each sentence element to other elements and to the whole sentence must be clear.*

We often see this principle violated with the careless use of an appositive. An appositive is a word or phrase that immediately follows another word or phrase and helps to define or identify it. In "George Washington, our first president, never told a lie," "our first president" stands in apposition to "George Washington." When the appositive does not immediately follow, the effect can be jarring to the reader. Sentences like this are common: "Jones stood next to the shiny new Jaguar, a tall, angular man with a large gold ring in his nose."

Negative appositives are especially prone to be misplaced: "The federal government is responsible for regulating securities, not the states." Obviously, the negative appositive "not the states" should immediately follow "federal government" for the relationship between the elements to be unmistakable.

Violation of this principle is most often the result of haste, not ignorance, on the part of the writer. It also comes from inept use of punctuation and from packing too much information into one sentence, which we will discuss at some length in "A Ten-Minute Writing Lesson."

Now let's look at some examples of sinful syntax and how the sentences might be revised:

• A pharmaceutical company newsletter, describing a new drug, reported, "The oral formulation will be particularly useful [for] patients who have difficulty swallowing tablets and children."

A writer with a sensitive ear for syntax would immediately discern that *children* is misplaced. As the sentence is written, *children* appears to be the object of *swallowing*. Any of three revisions would be acceptable:

1. "The oral formulation will be particularly useful for patients, including children, who have difficulty swallowing tablets."

2. "The oral formulation will be particularly useful for patients who have difficulty swallowing tablets, and for children."

3. "The oral formulation will be particularly useful for children and for patients who have difficulty swallowing tablets."

• From the *Atlanta Constitution*: "[Senator Sam Nunn] said earlier this year that he would decide whether to form an exploratory committee—the first step in a presidential campaign—by the end of the month."

The reporter who wrote that sentence probably knew that what Senator Nunn said was that he would decide by the end of the month whether to form an exploratory committee. A reader might infer, especially on hurried reading, that the Senator was thinking about forming the committee by the end of the month. We might be accused of nit-picking by citing that sentence, which we admit would be clear to most readers. Nevertheless, even the slightest possibility of ambiguity would be eliminated with "by the end of the month" after *decide*, where it belongs.

• From an advertising brochure for Hartwell Medical Corp., Carlsbad, California: "Further, they have allowed us to splint the torsos of several patients we've required to fly in helicopters with unstable spinal injuries." The prepositional phrase "with unstable spinal injuries" is positioned as if it modified *helicopters*, in violation of the first principle named above. The phrase is meant to describe *patients*.

Our revision: "Further, they have allowed us to splint the torsos of several patients with unstable spinal injuries whom we've required to fly in helicopters."

Further, they have allowed us to splint the torsos of several patients we've required to fly in helicopters with unstable spinal injuries.

• A promotional ad for the *Chicago Tribune,* published in the newspaper's Sunday edition, bore this headline: AN OPPORTUNITY THAT ONLY COMES ONCE IN A LIFETIME. Misplacement of *only* is probably the most common syntactical fault in both speech and writing. In this example, *only* refers to *once,* not *comes:* "An Opportunity That Comes Only Once in a Lifetime."

The word *only* is especially bothersome to many writers. Moving it around in a sentence can cause subtle changes in meaning. The six sentences below differ only in the position of *only*. See whether you agree that the meaning of each is slightly different.

1. "Only John vowed to date Mary." (This is unambiguous. It means that John was the only person who vowed to date Mary.)

2. "John only vowed to date Mary." (Two meanings are possible: John was the only person who vowed to date Mary, or John vowed to date Mary, but that's all he did.)

3. "John vowed only to date Mary." (This could mean that to date Mary was the only vow John made.)

4. "John vowed to only date Mary." (This could imply that John vowed to date Mary, but not to marry her.)

5. "John vowed to date only Mary." (This is unambiguous.)

6. "John vowed to date Mary only." (This means the same as the previous sentence except that it is more emphatic. The end of a sentence has the greatest impact on the reader.)

• From a *New Yorker* magazine review of Henrik Ibsen's *The Doll House:* "Nora is a hubbub of Christmas preparation, and McTeer, who is a strapping, big-boned woman with a large sense of humor, swoops around the room like the woman-child she is—giggling, talking to herself, letting her tongue play across her lips, hiding the macaroons that are forbidden by Torvald under the piano lid."

What, we wonder, was Torvald doing under the piano lid? The reviewer let a long, unwieldy sentence get out of control and ended it with a misplaced modifier, the prepositional phrase, "under the piano lid," which belongs next to *hiding*.

A possible revision: "Nora is a hubbub of Christmas preparation. McTeer, a strapping, big-boned woman with a large sense of humor, swoops around the room like the woman-child she is—giggling, talking to herself, letting her tongue play across her lips. She hides, under the piano lid, the macaroons that are forbidden by Torvald."

• From a news report on radio station KMPH, Fresno, California: "Neighbors fought the fire before firefighters arrived with a garden hose." One would think that firefighters in Fresno would bring more than a garden hose to a fire. We suggest "Neighbors fought the fire with a garden hose before firefighters arrived."

• From the *Sun,* San Bernardino, California: "Police say an Antioch man has admitted to killing his pregnant wife and daughter in an interview with police." Did the man kill his wife and daughter during the interview? Were both the wife and daughter pregnant? Suggested revision: "Police say an Antioch man admitted during an interview that he killed his daughter and his pregnant wife."

Here are nine additional examples. We recommend that you revise them to improve their syntax:

1. "Officer Niles Sherman, who was first to arrive, said he spied Ayers plunging a knife into Hollier through an open window." *(The Los Angeles Daily News)*

2. "On a quiet block of Talbot Avenue where power lines are the only relief to the endless blue sky, Gaskin deposited a flyer inviting residents to plant a tree in mail boxes and under doors." *(The Albany* [New York] *Journal)*

3. "When I entered the sand area, I noticed a person on the sandbar at a greater distance, wearing what looked like a blue jacket with a beard." (From the transcript of testimony in a case heard in Washington, North Carolina.)

4. "She was the only woman who changed for the wedding of Jack and Jackie in the rest room of a gas station." (From a column by nationally syndicated columnist Ellen Goodman.)

5. "Deanna M. Fairchild, 41, [is] accused of setting a fire in a rural neighborhood that killed three people." *(The Miami Herald)*

6. "Ron Brown was remembered as . . . a defender of little people who enjoyed being chauffeured around in limousines. . . ." *(Time)*

7. "About two hours later, Sillar returned to the demonstration and severely beat two men videotaping the demonstration with a flashlight." *(The San Francisco Daily Journal)*

8. "Secretary of State Warren Christopher (left) and Defense Secretary William Perry testify about chemical weapons on Capitol Hill recently." (Photo caption in the *Orlando Sentinel.*)

9. YOUNGSTER SHOT WHILE RIDING DETROIT SCHOOL BUS OUT OF HOSPITAL. (Headline in the *Grand Rapids Press.*)

One of the popular items that circulate through the network of folk xerography and E-mail is a perverse set of "fumblerules" along the lines of "Thimk," "We Never Make Misteaks," and "Plan Ahe—" (and then the space runs out)—injunctions that call attention to the very mistakes they seek to enjoin. English teachers and journalists have been passing around a list of self-contradictory rules of usage for more than a century, and we've been collecting and creating them for almost half of one.

Now, as a lighthearted review of English usage, we can offer you one of the largest accumulations of fumblerules ever gathered into a single space. Whatever you think of these slightly cracked nuggets of rhetorical wisdom, just remember that all generalizations are bad.

Fifty rules for writing good

1. Each pronoun should agree with their antecedent.
2. Between you and I, pronoun case is important.
3. A writer must be sure to avoid using sexist pronouns in his writing.
4. Verbs has to agree with their subjects.
5. Don't be a person whom people realize confuses *who* and *whom*.
6. Never use no double negatives.
7. Never use a preposition to end a sentence with. That is something up with which your readers will not put.
8. When writing, participles must not be dangled.
9. Be careful to never, under any circumstances, split infinitives.
10. Hopefully, you won't float your adverbs.
11. A writer must not shift your point of view.
12. Lay down and die before using a transitive verb without an object.
13. Join clauses good, like a conjunction should.
14. The passive voice should be avoided.
15. About sentence fragments.
16. Don't verb nouns.
17. In letters themes reports and ad copy use commas to separate items in a series.

18. Don't use commas, that aren't necessary.
19. "Don't overuse 'quotation marks.' "
20. Parenthetical remarks (however relevant) are (if the truth be told) superfluous.
21. Contractions won't, don't, and can't help your writing voice.
22. Don't write run-on sentences they are hard to read.
23. Don't forget to use end punctuation
24. Its important to use apostrophe's in the right places.
25. Don't abbrev.
26. Don't overuse exclamation marks!!!
27. Resist Unnecessary Capitalization.
28. Avoid mispellings.
29. Check to see if you any words out.
30. One-word sentences? Never.
31. Avoid annoying, affected, and awkward alliteration, always.
32. Never, ever use repetitive redundancies.
33. The bottom line is to bag trendy locutions that sound flaky.
34. By observing the distinctions between adjectives and adverbs, you will treat your readers real good.
35. Parallel structure will help you in writing more effective sentences and to express yourself more gracefully.
36. In our own personal opinion at this point of time, we think that authors, when they are writing, should not get into the habit of making use of too many unnecessary words that they don't really need.
37. Foreign words and phrases are the reader's beet noire and are not apropos.
38. Who needs rhetorical questions?
39. Always go in search for the correct idiom.
40. Do not cast statements in the negative form.
41. And don't start sentences with conjunctions.
42. Avoid mixed metaphors. They will kindle a flood of confusion in your readers.

43. Eliminate quotations. As Ralph Walled Emerson said, "I hate quotations. Tell me what you know."
44. Analogies in writing are like feathers on a snake.
45. Go around the barn at high noon to avoid colloquialisms.
46. Be more or less specific.
47. If I've told you once, I've told you a thousand times, exaggeration is a billion times worse than understatement, which is always best.
48. Never use a big word when you can utilize a diminutive word.
49. Profanity sucks.
50. Last but not least, even if you have to bend over backward, avoid clichés like the plague.

VI

Grammar Games

One summer one of your faithful grammar watchdogs picked up a discount coupon for Benson's Animal Park in southern New Hampshire. One crucial sentence in the document read: "This coupon is good for $2.00 off the regular admission price for each member of your family."

The author was puzzled about the exact meaning of the offer. Was Benson's promising him a $2.00 discount for all members of his family whom he brought to the park, or did he need a coupon for each member? Just in case the second meaning prevailed, the watchdog author snatched up a coupon for each member of his party, but when he stepped up to the Benson's ticket office, he found that he needed only one coupon for everybody. "This coupon is good for $2.00 off the regular admission price for *all* members of your family" would have avoided confusion.

Once inside the animal park, the author and family man saw this sign in the sea lions' area: PLEASE DO NOT THROW ANYTHING IN THE POOL. "How bizarre," he thought. "Why would anybody think that I could or would want to toss around a sea lion?" "Please Do Not Throw Anything into the Pool" would have been clearer.

The difference a word makes

To discover how a slight difference in wording can make a vast difference in meaning, examine each pair of sentences and choose the one that answers the question correctly. Answers appear in the Answers section:

1. Which baseball player has wings?
   a. The batter flew out to left field.
   b. The batter flied out to left field.

2. Which judge would you prefer?
   a. At the trial the judge was completely uninterested.
   b. At the trial the judge was completely disinterested.

3. Which students received a special exemption?
   a. The draft board excepted all students.
   b. The draft board accepted all students.

4. Which people had met previously?
   a. We were formally introduced.
   b. We were formerly introduced.

5. Which Pat is a girl?
   a. Pat was smarter than the boys in the class.
   b. Pat was smarter than the other boys in the class.

6. Which request would parents be more likely to make to their children?
   a. Bring the stray dog home.
   b. Take the stray dog home.

7. Which runner put her foot down?
   a. She hoped to reach the finish line.
   b. She hopped to reach the finish line.

8. Which dog is definitely not a bloodhound?
   a. The dog smelled badly.
   b. The dog smelled bad.

9. Which Hood was careless?
   a. In tight situations, Robin Hood tended to loose arrows.
   b. In tight situations, Robin Hood tended to lose arrows.

10. Which newspapers are dishonest?
    a. The newspapers lied about the back room of the casino.
    b. The newspapers lay about the back room of the casino.

11. Which person can see the sky?
    a. The camper lay prone on the grass.
    b. The camper lay supine on the grass.

12. Which child is afflicted with a defect?
    a. Mother went shopping with her toe-headed son.
    b. Mother went shopping with her towheaded son.

13. Which caveman liked the company of others?
    a. Ug found a club.
    b. Ug founded a club.

14. Which John is a thespian?
    a. John acted as an old man.
    b. John acted like an old man.

15. Which speaker is smarter?
    a. In the room were four geniuses beside me.
    b. In the room were four geniuses besides me.

16. Which twosome is playing doubles?
    a. Ellen complemented Frank's tennis game.
    b. Ellen complimented Frank's tennis game.

17. Which is the greater compliment?
    a. I know you're superior.
    b. I know your superior.

18. Which leader is more resourceful?
    a. The mayor adapted her predecessor's policies.
    b. The mayor adopted her predecessor's policies.

19. Which town probably has the stronger school system?
    a. I admire the town's principles.
    b. I admire the town's principals.

20. Which student will receive the higher grade?
    a. His answers were all most accurate.
    b. His answers were almost accurate.

21. In which case is Phil cashing in on his father's power?
    a. Phil flaunts his father's authority.
    b. Phil flouts his father's authority.

22. Which person is more skeptical?
    a. She is an incredible reader.
    b. She is an incredulous reader.

23. Which invitation is more dangerous?
    a. I invite you to desert.
    b. I invite you to dessert.

24. Which structure got bombed?
    a. The soldiers raised a fort.
    b. The soldiers razed a fort.

25. Which statement has a sock in it?
    a. It's darned good.
    b. It's darned well.

26. Which marriage is stronger?
    a. My wife likes golf better than I.
    b. My wife likes golf better than me.

27. Which man could be called a Romeo?
    a. He spent a lot of time repelling women.
    b. He spent a lot of time repulsing women.

28. Which speaker is more likely to be a magician?
    a. She embellished her talk with a series of allusions.
    b. She embellished her talk with a series of illusions.

She embellished her talk with a series of illusions.

29. In which situation should you be careful about lighting a match?
    a. In the room stood a tank of inflammable gas.
    b. In the room stood a tank of nonflammable gas.

30. Which person was not invited to the party?
    a. They left me out of the party.
    b. They let me out of the party.

31. Which boy is angry at his sisters?
    a. He called his sisters names.
    b. He called his sisters' names.

32. Which is worse for the Democratic Party?
    a. Democrats who are seen as weak will not be elected.
    b. Democrats, who are seen as weak, will not be elected.

33. Which private is more nervous?
    a. Shaking with fear, the major reprimanded the private.
    b. Shaking with fear, the private was reprimanded by the major.

34. Which finder is a prisoner?
    a. Locked in a cell, he discovered the jewels.
    b. He discovered the jewels locked in a cell.

35. Which statement definitely contains two people?
    a. Mary implied that she was unhappy with the job.
    b. Mary inferred that she was unhappy with the job.

For the idea of this game and for some of the examples we are indebted to Maxwell Nurnberg, *Questions you always wanted to ask about English but were afraid to raise your hand* (Washington Square Press, 1972).

A comedy of errors

Language errors can slither into all sorts of territory—books, newspapers, magazines, advertisements, student essays, church notes, radio and television broadcasts—everywhere. Alas, the grammar gremlins can also show their mischievous faces in our beloved comic strips, which afford us no comic relief from the boo-boos and bloopers, fluffs and flubs, and goofs and gaffes that plague the printed page. Because words within comic strip panels and cartoons are usually hand-lettered, errors in usage can't be written off as mere typos. We do wonder if these not-so-comic goofs and gaffes affect the way our young people read and write.

In the punny comic strip "Frank and Ernest," the two baggy funny guys are standing in a sand trap at a golf course and Frank grumbles at Ernest, "You humming 'Mr. Sandman' isn't helping any!"

In "Blondie," Herb says to Dagwood, "I sure appreciate you making the bookcase for me, Dag."

In "Funky Winkerbean," the Mrs. asks, "Honey . . . What do you think about me taking some courses at Kent this fall?"

And in "Pickles," the old fellow sighs to his grandson: "One good thing about me being wrong—It brings such joy to your grandma."

In all four examples, the speakers violate the rule that calls for a possessive pronoun before a gerund, a rule that we discussed in the first chapter of this book. *Your* and *my* would have been more graceful and acceptable in the four instances than *you* and *me*.

"You can't ask for formal English in comic strips," you may well protest. But this isn't formal English; it's simply correct English. For example, in Robb Armstrong's "Jump Start," a little six- or seven-year-old boy says, smilingly, "I appreciate your taking time away from your vacation to bandage my head." Congratters, kid, you got the possessive pronoun right, even if the adults in the other strips didn't.

Here are fifty quotations from various widely circulated strips. Identify the breach of English usage that afflicts each item. Check your answers in the Answers section:

1. Sir Rodney sweats profusely as he looks at a sign that reads ARENA TODAY/SLAUGHTER AT IT'S BEST.—"The Wizard of Id"

2. Mr. Dithers to Mrs. Dithers: "Look at the money we save each year by using less and less candles on your cake."—"Blondie"

3. Bouncing a basketball off Linus's head, Lucy shouts, "I'm gonna try out for the girl's basketball team."—"Peanuts"

4. Senator: "It is indeed true that on one occasion I did refer to our reception person as a quote, *fabulous babe,* unquote."—"Shoe"

5. "Well, for the third millenium in a row, no Las Vegas night."—"Porterfield"

6. Lawyer to peasant lying on the pavement: "If you crawl ten

feet further, I'll make a few bucks for both of us."—"The Wizard of Id"

7. "The great astronomer Carl Sagan scans the heavens . . . taking in the enormity of the universe."—"Bloom County"

8. "Yep! According to the male bonding rule book, it's okay for you and I to embrace in a full bear hug."—"Jump Start"

9. "Neither the Lord nor myself need any more grocery coupons."—"The Wizard of Id"

10. "The great thing about a garden hose is that it lays there all coiled up in the grass, silent, motionless, just like a snake, But when you step on it . . . it doesn't bite."—"Bizarro"

11. Peppermint Patty: "Not quite the same with you and I, ma'am?"—"Peanuts"

12. King: "All for one and one for all! We are no different than any other team!"—"The Wizard of Id"

13. Frank: "I always check Ernie's alphabet soup to make sure there's no four letter words in it."—"Frank and Ernest"

14. Voice on television: "And, since using Blockade, I haven't seen any more fleas on Buster . . . and there's none on his dog neither . . ."—"Shoe"

15. "This is the tree where me and my very first sweetheart carved our initials."—"Broom-Hilda"

16. Little brother fish to his piscine sister: "Your blind date's here, and it's one of those kind with the eyes bugged way out!"—"The Far Side"

17. "Would you recommend red or white wine to compliment 'mystery meat'?"—"Shoe"

18. "No, but I could aggravate the heck out of him."—"Shoe"

19. Nancy to Sluggo: "We have two classes coming in here for the movie . . . Can I sit in your lap?"—"Nancy"

20. "Things aren't exactly as they were before! Any more unexpected changes and I may just get nauseous!!"—"Bloom County"

21. Peasant pointing at a speaker's stand: "What's the podium

for?" Government official: "That's where the King works out."—"The Wizard of Id"

22. "Yes, regular employees are paid less than contract employees such as yourself."—"Dilbert"

23. "So this is just more evidence that the corporate paper shufflers in control of America's great creative mediums are a bumbling bunch of boneheads."—"Bloom County"

24. Sarge: "Beetle, go put up this target. The General is anxious to do some rifle practice."—"Beetle Bailey"

25. "Muffin likes to act all hoity-toity, like she's better than us."—"Marvin"

26. Man responding to another man who is looking at his tattoo: "It's my PIN number, Mr. Nosy."—"Non-Sequitur"

27. "To whither doest thou go, dear pilgrim?"—"Bloom County"

28. Beetle: "Why do I always have to do what you say?!" Sarge: "Because I'm the head honcho and you're the poor peon."—"Beetle Bailey"

29. Postman: "I'll play it safe this morning and wait in the Woodley's yard until Bumstead is gone."—"Blondie"

30. Nancy walks past various signs in a clothing store: WOMEN'S FASHIONS, MISSES' FASHIONS, JUNIOR'S FASHIONS.—"Nancy"

31. "That is, it's designed to insure that, once and for all, our successors clean up their act."—"Shoe"

32. "Oh. I thought you were effecting an English accent."—"Miss Peach"

33. "Splendid. I, Cutter John, . . . new arrival to this wilderness called Bloom County, now finds himself hurtling toward oblivion."—"Bloom County"

34. Snoopy typing "Cooking Hints": "When mixing dog food in a bowl, the water can either be put in first or added last."—"Peanuts"

35. "I have a simple rule for hunting, son . . . Only shoot what you're gonna eat."—"Shoe"

36. Coach to kids: "The reason we never win is because you never

get the ball in the basket . . . which, after all, is the whole idea of the game."—"Miss Peach"

37. In one of his fantasies, Calvin stares out from a spaceship at a barren planetscape and says, "What strange chemicals must compose this alien soil! Crossing a rift, the rocks abruptly change color."—"Calvin and Hobbes"

38. B.D. and Boopsie have a reunion after B.D.'s 242 days as a soldier in Desert Shield and Desert Storm. They look at each other and simultaneously exclaim, "It was hardest on me."—"Doonesbury"

39. Mom receives four red roses for Mother's Day. "Roses! They're lovely," she exclaims. "Four red ones to symbolize Mike, Liz, April, and I," explains her husband. "And one beautiful yellow one to represent you!"—"For Better or for Worse"

40. "Just think, Joey . . . If the stork had landed two more houses further, you'd be my little brother!"—"Dennis the Menace"

41. Zonker asks Doonesbury, "How goes the Muzak wars today?"—"Doonesbury"

42. Nancy sighs, "I wish I was better looking." "Don't worry about it," Sluggo counsels. "Maybe you're one of those people who's beautiful on the inside."—"Nancy"

43. Cookie: "Daddy just had a pizza delivered." Alexander: "Great! Daddy orders more toppings than anyone in the world!" Cookie: "Well, this time he outdid himself." Alexander: "Why do you say that?" The two children stare as Dagwood enters the room directing two pizza men lugging a huge vat labeled "Pizzaria."—"Blondie"

44. When a friend asks her, "Of which political party are you a member, Rose?" Rose replies, "The 'I agree with whomever is speaking' party!"—"Rose Is Rose"

45. As her young son jerks and yowls in her arms, Mom says to her brother, "I thought you'd sit around with us for awhile and relax!"—"For Better or for Worse"

46. When Winky tells Missy, "I just seen a asternut on T.V.,"

Mother corrects him, saying, "I *saw* an astronaught, Winky."—"The Ryatts"

47. "Gail Burke of Dallas, Texas, says her cat Duffy is the family librarian. The trick is to try and take a book without waking up Duffy."—"Heathcliff"

48. Dogbert: "I will now use my power of cute ears to abuse the banking industry. I'd like to make a large withdrawal from other peoples' accounts."—"Dilbert"

49. "With their last child off to college, the keys to the mini van are revoked."—"Nest Heads"

50. A pack of dogs is driving down the street in a big car. Suddenly, one of the canines, with a rope around his neck, flies out of the car. The caption explains: "Careening through the neighborhood with reckless abandon, none of them suspected that Tuffy was still tied up."—"The Far Side"

VII

Help for the Orthographically Challenged

One night when Joel Chandler Harris, creator of the Uncle Remus tales, was at his editorial desk, an old-time reporter looked over and asked, "Say, Joel, how do you spell the word *graphic*? With one *f* or two *f*'s?"

"Well," replied Harris in his gentle drawl, "if you're going to use any *f*'s, you might as well go the limit."

We may smile at the reporter's question, yet who among us has not stumbled into the potholes and booby traps that pock the terrain of English spelling? If we try to spell words by the way they sound, we will surely misspell many of them. But who among us is gifted with such vastness of visual memory that we can spell words solely by the eye?

In the long-ago days before tobacco became the epitome of evil, there was a brand of cigarettes called Pall Mall. Pall Malls came in an attractive red package and were one of the first, if not the first, of the king-size brands. In those days cigarette advertising on television was permitted, and we can visualize even now the mellow-voiced Frank Blair on the *Today* show extolling "Pall Mall Famous Cigarettes." He sounded their name as "Pell Mell," which is how our British cousins pronounce the name of the famous London street from which the cigarettes presumably took their name.

Americans, for the most part unfamiliar with London thoroughfares, called the fags "Pawl Mawls," and a noted graffito expressed the Americans' disdain for the niceties of British pronunciation: "Pall Mall can't spall."

Come to think of it, why would anyone pronounce something "pell mell" and spell it "pall mall"? Perhaps for the same reason that we call a train station a "depo" and spell it "depot" or that a bass can be a fiddle or a fish, or a bow can be found on ship or on a gaily wrapped Christmas package.

That popular author named Unknown, whose work makes the rounds of the Internet and folk xerography circuits, contributes the following insight into the tangles of English orthography:

Our Queer Language

When the English tongue we speak,
Why is *break* not rhymed with *freak*?
Will you tell me why it's true
That we say *sew* but likewise *few*?

And the maker of a verse
Cannot rhyme his *horse* with *worse*?
Beard sounds not the same as *heard*.
And *cord* is different from *word*.

Cow is *cow*, and low is *low*.
Shoe is never rhymed with *foe*.
Think of *rose* and *close* and *lose*,
And think of *goose* and yet of *choose*.

Think of *comb* and *tomb* and *bomb*,
Doll and *roll* and *home* and *some*,
And since *pay* is rhymed with *say*,
Why not *paid* with *said*, I pray?

We have *blood* and *food* and *good*.
Cough is not pronounced like *could*.
Wherefore *done* but *gone* and *lone*?
Is there any reason known?

I shall wonder ever after
Why *slaughter* doesn't rhyme with *laughter*.
Thus, in short, it seems to me
Sounds and letters disagree.

It is a remarkable fact that English, now the language most widely used for international trade, aviation, science, travel, and political affairs, is the most orthographically challenging of all written languages. A Spanish schoolchild likely would find the idea of a spelling bee quaint, for most Spanish words are pronounced as they are spelled. Would that the same were true for English. But it isn't, and anyone who wants to use English correctly must learn to spell.

Spelling is like penmanship. When it's good, you receive no extra credit. When it's bad, you run into trouble. Some people seem to be naturally good spellers, but most people have to learn a spell of good

English. You can acquire spelling ability provided you are willing to build your skill and have a will to learn.

Bad spellers are not necessarily dunderheads. George Washington, reporting a shortage of provisions, wrote: "With respect to the Flower we find our Necessaties are not such as to require an immediate Transportation during the Harvist." He wrote "flagg" for *flag*, "ingagement" for *engagement*, and "centry" for *sentry*. President Andrew Jackson once blew his stack while trying to compose a presidential paper. "It's a damned poor mind that can think of only one way to spell a word," he thundered. Vice President Dan Quayle was widely ridiculed for having told a schoolchild that *potato* was spelled "potatoe." When the spelling bugbears are biting you, think of George Washington, Andrew Jackson, and Dan Quayle and know that you're not alone.

Well, you might say, spelling is no problem today. We have spell checkers on our word processors. That's like saying that doctors became unnecessary with the discovery of aspirin. Spell checkers are wonderful for catching typographical errors and some misspellings, but they can be a mixed blessing if they make writers overconfident. Kerry Wood, a teacher from California, assigned his students to write a paper on *Othello*. One student's paper referred to "Testimonial" and "Yahoo" as characters in the play. Puzzled at first, Mr. Wood finally surmised that the student had relied on the spell checker, which had failed to recognize the names of two of Shakespeare's most memorable characters—Desdemona and Iago—and, as spell checkers are wont to do, "corrected" the student's spelling as best it could. The student failed to check the checker.

Here's a sampling of other student spelling blunders that were not caught by any spell checker:

- Joan of Arc was burnt to a steak.
- To celebrate at feasts, the inhabitants of Old England sometimes cut the head off the biggest bore and carried it around on a platter.

- They gave William IV a lovely funeral. It took six men to carry the beer.
- On Thanksgiving morning we could smell the foul cooking.
- In Pittsburgh, they manufacture iron and steal.

On Thanksgiving morning we could smell the foul cooking.

The main problem with spell checkers is that they cannot distinguish between or among homophones, which are words that sound alike but have different meanings, such as *role/roll, deer/dear, alter/altar,* and *to/too/two.*

The hazards of relying on the spell checker are well illustrated in the following poem, which has made the rounds on the Internet for several years, in one variation or another:

AN OWED TO THE SPELL CHECKER

Wee have a spelling checker.
It came with hour PC.
It plane lee marks four are revue
Miss steaks wee can knot sea.

Weave run this poem threw it.
Your sure reel pleas two no.
Its vary polished inn it's weigh.
Hour checker tolled me sew.

A checker is a bless sing,
It freeze yew lodes of thyme.
It helps me right awl stiles two reed,
And aides me when aye rime.

Each frays come posed up on my screen
Eye trussed two bee a joule.
The checker pours oar every word
To cheque sum spelling rule.

Bee fore a veiling checkers
Hour spelling mite decline,
And if we're lacks oar have a laps,
Wee wood bee maid to wine.

Butt now bee cause hour spelling
Is checked with such grate flare,
Their are know faults with inn my cite,
Of nun eye am a wear.

Now, spelling does knot phase us,
It does knot bring a tier.
My pay purrs awl due glad den
With wrapped words fare as hear.

Too rite with care is quite a feet
Of witch won should bee proud.
And wee mussed dew the best whee can,
Four flaws are knot aloud.

Sew ewe can sea why whee dew prays
Such soft wear four pea seas,
And why wee brake inn two averse
Buy righting want too pleas.

Jerrold H. Zar, dean of the Graduate School of Northern Illinois University, composed the poem as an extension of a two-verse poem by Mark Eckman, of Morristown, New Jersey. According to Dean Zar's count, 123 of the poem's 225 words are incorrect, but all passed muster with his spell checker. Incidentally, if we were relying on our spell checker, Jerrold Zar's name would be Jailed Zaire.

So perhaps the first rule for better spelling ought to be this: If you have a spell checker, use it; but don't ask it to do something it was never designed to do.

Beyond that, here are nine other suggestions that can help the orthographically challenged to be less so:

(2) *Develop your visual memory*. It is impossible to spell by ear alone. When you read, pay attention to how words are spelled and how they differ from other words that have the same or similar combinations of letters. You can also develop visual memory by using flash cards, which are available commercially. The flash cards we have seen are intended as vocabulary builders. Each card has a word and its pronunciation on one side and its definition on the other. Thus, they can help you to improve both your spelling and your vocabulary.

(3) *Become familiar with the most common spelling demons*. Dr. Thomas Clark Pollock, of New York University, has been working for decades on a study of the most common misspellings by high school and college students. Dr. Pollock found that just nine words account for more than 7 percent of mistakes in the test. These devilish demons are: *their (there), too (to), receive, believe (belief), all right, separate, coming, until*, and *character*.

In order of the frequency of their misspelling, here is the second battalion of spelling demons:

definite	appearance
writing	necessary
whether	convenience
interest	thought
occurrence/occurred	principal/principle
decide	criticism
privilege	probably
tried/tries	quiet
description	realize
beginning	rhythm
finally	acquainted
humorous	clothes
occasion	describe
friend	stopped
disappoint	than
recommend	experience
women	immediately

(4) *Make a list of the words that are especially troublesome to you.* Words that bother others might not bother you, and vice versa, but the most pesky gremlins are the ones that trouble you. One of the authors of this book confesses that he sometimes puts a *u* in *forty* and an extra *e* in *judgment,* although he's never bothered by such spelling demons as *separate* and *cemetery*.

Keep a copy of your list close at hand and refer to it when you write. Tape-record it and listen to the tape as you drive to work. Make and use a set of flash cards with the words on your list.

With these and other activities you might devise on your own, the correct spellings of the words that bug you should soon become second nature. You can also improve your spelling by writing the words on your "trouble list" over and over until the motions required are automatic. In sports, this is called "muscle memory." By performing a motion repeatedly, you develop the ability to perform it without conscious effort.

(5) *Become especially conscious of homophones.* In just the first stanza of "An Owed to the Spell Checker," above, we find the homophones *we/wee/whee, our/hour, plane/plain, knot/not, stakes/steaks, four/for/fore, revue/review,* and *sea/see.* Many books of grammar and usage, including our previous book, *The Write Way,* contain lists of homophones. Scanning a list of sound-alikes and look-alikes will fix certain homophones in your mind. When you encounter a word that's one of a homophonic pair or trio, you will be warned to look it up if you're not certain that the choice you see is the right one.

(6) *When in doubt about the spelling of any word, look it up in your dictionary.* Own a reliable, up-to-date dictionary and use it constantly. The English language boasts the largest and finest dictionaries in the world. The average time for locating a word in the dictionary is twenty seconds, surely twenty seconds well spent. There is no disgrace in not knowing a spelling, only in not caring enough to go to a little extra trouble to get it right.

(7) *Master a few basic spelling rules.* Skillful spellers have the good sense to learn and apply a relatively small number of fundamental spelling rules, each of which pertains to a large number of words.

You know, of course, that *write* ends with an *e* and that the *e* disappears in *writing.* The same rule applies to the likes of *dine/dining* and *come/coming.* Drop the final *e* before a suffix beginning with a vowel:

hope/hoping **line/lining** **shine/shining** **use/using**

Exceptions:

canoeing changeable noticeable singeing

Keep the final *e* before a suffix beginning with a consonant:

definite/definitely hope/hopeless state/statement use/useful

Exceptions:

acknowledgment argument duly judgment ninth

When the suffixes *ness* and *ly* are added to a word, the spelling of the word usually remains the same:

casual/casually mean/meanness

But words ending in *y* change the *y* to *i* before a suffix:

beauty/beautiful happy/happily

Change a final *y* preceded by a consonant to *i* before any suffix that does not begin with *i:*

ally/alliance baby/babies clumsy/clumsiness happy/happier

Words ending in *ie* drop the *e* and change the *i* to *y* before adding *ing* to avoid two *i*'s in a row:

die/dying lie/lying tie/tying

Note: *dye/dyeing* to distinguish from *die/dying*.

The next rule—about what to do with final consonants—will help you to spell thousands of words.

Why is the verb *scar* spelled with one *r*—and *scarred* and *scarring* spelled with two? Doubling the *r* keeps the sound of the vowel *a* from changing. Without doubling the *r* before adding *ed* or *ing*, the *a* would have the sound of the *a* in *scare,* instead of the *a* sound in *scar*.

For words ending in a single consonant preceded by a single vowel, double the final consonant *if* the word is accented on the last syllable. This includes all one-syllable words ending with a single vowel and then a consonant:

bat/batted drag/dragging mop/mopped pin/pinned

as well as all such words of two syllables or more:

admit/admitting occur/occurrence prefer/preferred

If the accent does not fall on the final syllable of the root word, the consonant is not doubled:

benefit/benefited profit/profiting travel/traveler

There once was a young Puritan man who had a great deal of difficulty remembering the various rules of conduct in his community. He tried hard, but was constantly being ridiculed because of some breach of etiquette. In desperation, he asked an older man to teach him proper manners. The task was formidable, and the older man's patience grew thin, as he had to chastise the younger man repeatedly for his awkward ways.

Finally, on the way into church one Sunday, the younger man started into the building ahead of the older man. He was firmly collared by his elder, who then allowed a lady to go in ahead of both of them. The young man expressed his regret.

The older, losing his temper, screamed, "Canst thou remember nothing? How much easier can it become?" Pointing out the woman who had just entered, he said, "It is I before Thee, except after She!"

This, of course, is a set-up pun on the best known of all spelling jingles:

I before *E,*
Except after *C,*
Or when sounded as *A,*
As in *neighbor* and *weigh.*

You don't have to be an *Einstein* to realize that the *i*-before-*e* rule is breached as often as it is observed. If you want to find out just how many proper names violate the rule, remember this sentence: "Eugene *O'Neill* and Dwight *Eisenhower* drank a 35-degree-*Fahrenheit Budweiser* and *Reingold* in *Anaheim* and *Leicester.*" Nor do you have to be an Einstein to see that *Einstein* itself is a double violation of the *i*-before-*e* rule (along with *Weinstein, Feinstein, deficiencies, efficiencies, proficiencies,* and *zeitgeist*).

Among the many instances in which *e* precedes *i* in uncapitalized words are this dozen: *caffeine, kaleidoscope, counterfeit, leisure, either, protein, feisty, seize, heifer, sovereign, height,* and *therein.*

And among words in which *c* is immediately followed by *ie* we note *ancient, omniscient, concierge, science, conscience, society, fancier, species, financier, sufficient, glacier,* and *tendencies.*

Taking the fullest of breaths, we hope that a full statement of the rule for spelling *ie* and *ei* words will be of some help to you:

I before *e*
When the sound is long *e*
(With some exceptions).
I after *e,*

Especially after *c*,
When the sound is long *e*
(With some exceptions).

(8) *Learn or create some basic mnemonic devices.* In an old movie the gruff and grizzled newspaper editor finds his star reporter dead drunk in the bar as a big story is about to break. An enterprising young kid, played by Spencer Tracy, jumps up and asks for the assignment.

"Do you have any experience?" asks the editor.
"No," replies the kid.
"Spell parallel," growls the editor.
"P-a-r-a-l-l-e-l," spells the kid, and he gets the big story.

How did the kid know how to spell *parallel*? He remembered to employ a mnemonic device he had been taught in grade school. He thought of *ll* as railroad tracks, which are parallel, running through the middle of a town. This reminded him that *parallel* is not spelled "paralel" or "paralell."

You have just witnessed a mnemonic device in (lights, camera) action. A mnemonic device (the word is pronounced nee-MON-ic) is a concise, efficient memory jogger.

If *parallel* is one of your trouble words, try the mnemonic above. With a little imagination, you can come up with a memory device for almost any word by associating the word with something familiar. A good idea is to make up a device for each word on your list. That process itself will help you to recall the correct spelling of the words, and you will find your list shrinking.

Remember that there is *science* in *conscience, finite* in *definite, iron* in the *environment*, a *minus* in *minuscule*, a *pal* in *principal*, a *cog* in *recognize*, a *pet* in *repetition*, and *a rat* in *separate*.

(9) *Master the art and craft of capitalization.* To spell correctly, you must know not only which letters to use in words but which words should begin with capital letters. The rules are simple:

• Capitalize all proper nouns:

Albuquerque   Ethel   France   September

• Capitalize most adjectives formed from proper nouns:

Alaskan   French   Persian   Victorian

• Capitalize common nouns, which ordinarily are not capitalized, when they become part of a proper noun:

Good Shepherd Hospital   Missouri River   Oak Street

• Capitalize the first word, last word, and all important words in titles of books, magazines, newspapers, stories, articles, plays, and poems:

"The Rape of the Lock"   *The Song of the South*   *Time in a Bottle*

(10) *Learn the rules for compound words.* To compound (not confound) this discussion, we'll address a question that we're frequently asked: How should compounds be written?

Compound words may be variously styled as two words (open styling, as in *high school*), one word (solid, as in *highway*) or hyphenated (as in *sit-in*).

When in doubt about how to write a compound, consult your dictionary, making sure that dictionary is up to date. As usage guru Mary Louise Gilman explains, "Not only do new words come into the language at a dizzying pace, but the way we write old words changes. There's an ever-growing tendency to convert into a single word what we used to hyphenate or write as two or more words. I doubt if we'll ever approach the Germans in this respect, but we're tending [in] that direction."

Bearing in mind that dictionaries occasionally disagree with each other about how to write compounds and that there are exceptions to every rule of compounding, we offer the following generalities:

- Grammatical context often influences styling. Writers write *every day* because deadlines are *everyday* events to them. *Backdoor* schemes don't always slither in through the *back door*.
- Compound nouns may be variously written as in *boy scout, tongue-lashing, spaceship*. The historical drift is toward solid styling. Compound nouns that contain adverbs as the second element are usually hyphenated: *drive-in, go-between*.
- There is likewise little consistency in the styling of compound verbs, although the general rule is that adverb + verb combinations are solid (*overdo, undervalue*) and verb + adverb combinations are open (*given up, make out*).
- Compound adjectives are usually hyphenated, as in *one-horse, narrow-minded,* and *blue-black,* but adverb + adjective compounds are usually solid: *uptight, forthcoming.*
- Compound pronouns, prepositions, and adverbs are always solid: *whoever, herself, upon, throughout, nevertheless, moreover.*

Dictionaries may not always be consistent, but you should be. When you choose a style for a given word, stick with it throughout your text.

The ultimate spelling quiz

During our combined eighty years as writers, editors, and teachers, your user-friendly *Dogs* authors have compiled a list of the hundred words that our readers and students have most consistently misspelled. We have a powerful hunch that many of the same words are among the spelling demons that you most fear and loathe.

Here is the list. Look it over and think about it carefully. Then circle each word that you find to be spelled incorrectly. When you are finished, compare your total with the one given on page 205:

1. accommodate
2. achieve
3. aggressive
4. all right
5. arctic
6. asinine
7. assassination
8. athlete
9. background
10. balloon
11. banana
12. basically
13. bastion
14. battalion
15. benefit
16. broccoli
17. business
18. calendar
19. category
20. ceiling
21. cemetery
22. character
23. coliseum
24. commitment
25. complexion
26. controversy
27. curiosity
28. definitely
29. description
30. despair
31. develop
32. dilemma
33. disappoint
34. dissipate
35. ecstasy
36. embarrass
37. environment
38. etiquette
39. exhilarated
40. existence
41. fluorescent
42. forgo
43. forty
44. gauge
45. grammar
46. harass
47. hypocrisy
48. imitate
49. immediately
50. independent
51. ingenious
52. innate

53. inoculate
54. judgment
55. liaison
56. liquefy
57. marshmallow
58. mayonnaise
59. metaphor
60. millennium
61. minuscule
62. mischievous
63. missile
64. misspell
65. moccasin
66. noticeable
67. occasion
68. occurrence
69. parallel
70. pastime
71. perseverance
72. pharaoh
73. pizzeria
74. poinsettia
75. precede
76. prejudice
77. privilege
78. proceed
79. professor
80. publicly
81. quandary
82. receive
83. recommend
84. renown
85. repetition
86. restaurateur
87. rhythm
88. sacrilegious
89. sentence
90. separate
91. silhouette
92. sophomore
93. souvenir
94. subtly
95. supersede
96. surprise
97. threshold
98. tragedy
99. truly
100. unnecessary

VIII

The Common Comma

PITYTHEPOORGREEKSANDROMANSWHOHADTOREADWRITINGTHATHADNEITHERPUNCTUATIONNORSPACEBETWEENWORDSANDLETTERSWERETHESAMESIZENOUPPERANDLOWERCASESASWEHAVETODAYITWASALMOSTIMPOSSIBLETOTELLWHEREASENTENCEBEGANANDENDEDTOMAKEMATTERSWORSESOMEEARLYWRITINGRANALTERNATELYFROMRIGHTTOLEFTANDLEFTTORIGHT

THEN SOMEONE CAME UP WITH THE IDEA OF SEPARATING

WORDS WITH A LITTLE BIT OF SPACE AND READING GOT SOMEWHAT EASIER Finally, some bright soul invented punctuation and perhaps began to use letters of different sizes for different purposes. All of us owe him or her a debt of gratitude, for without punctuation, as demonstrated above, reading would be hellish.

Of course, no one really "invented" punctuation as we know it and use it today. It simply evolved. The period probably came first, then the comma to indicate pauses, and later the more sophisticated marks that advanced even further the causes of order, clarity, and grace. If the passage with which we opened this section seems akin to what American intelligence officers must have experienced in breaking the Imperial Japanese code in World War II, think how it would be to read an entire book with no periods, commas, hyphens, colons, quotation marks, exclamation points, parentheses, paragraph indents, or capital letters.

Punctuation contributes to clarity and readability by establishing the relationship of the parts of a sentence to each other and to the whole sentence. Punctuation also helps to set the pace of the writing, and it contributes in no small way to meaning. To the Netherlands Chamber of Deputies was brought a motion "for the naturalization of Nathalie Bouwmeester, widow of Peter Bouwmeester and eighteen men." A deputy arose to inquire gravely whether it was in accord with public morals to grant naturalization to a woman who had buried nineteen husbands.

Officials soon discovered that there had been a clerical error in the drafting of the motion. A comma separating the appositive "widow of Peter Bouwmeester" from "eighteen men" had been omitted. The motion thus amended, naturalization was voted and granted to Nathalie Bouwmeester, and also to the eighteen men.

A fascinating anecdote illustrating the importance of the comma is told by William Safire, columnist for the *New York Times*. During the 1984 Republican Convention, the platform-writing committee was divided over the wording of a proposed tax plank. Party "pragmatists," led by Senator Robert Dole, wanted the party to appear to be against tax increases without committing itself never to raise taxes. The more conservative among the Republican faithful wanted the anti-tax plank to be unequivocally against all tax increases. The pragmatists came up with this proposed statement:

> We therefore oppose any attempt to increase taxes which would harm the recovery.

The use of *which* without a comma following *taxes* made the sentence ambiguous—purposely, one might assume. Was the clause *which would harm the recovery* defining or nondefining? Did the sentence mean the Republican Party was opposed to *any* attempt to increase *any* taxes, or only such taxes as would harm the recovery?

In any case, the conservatives knew their punctuation. They insisted on inserting a comma in front of *which,* giving the sentence a clear meaning but a different one from what their pragmatic friends intended. Incensed, one of the pragmatists threatened to "take that comma to the convention floor." But cooler heads prevailed and the conservatives won the day without a floor fight over a common comma. Is this a great country, or what?

That story, incidentally, also illustrates the pitfalls of introducing a defining clause with *which,* as we discussed in a previous chapter. If the pragmatists had used *that* rather than *which,* with no following comma, the clause would have been clearly defining and the meaning of the sentence unmistakable.

We do not in this chapter and the next offer a complete punctuation guide. In keeping with the overall theme of *Sleeping Dogs,* we simply discuss some of the most challenging and perplexing aspects of punctuation.

The comma is the most common punctuation mark and probably the most commonly misunderstood and misused. Its most important function is to indicate a natural pause. The writer who uses commas in that way, without bothering consciously to follow rules, will not be wrong often. One problem with that approach, however, is that a pause that is natural to one reader is not necessarily natural to another. The approach tends to result in more commas than modern writers like to use.

Some writers use commas to create certain effects or to emphasize points, just as a pause in speaking can be used for emphasis. Although too many commas can be distracting, it seems better, in the interest of clarity, to have too many rather than too few. In the comic strip "Mother Goose and Grim," Mother reprimands her dog, who is dragging into the room a young fellow. Eyes a-popping, she yells, "No, Grimmy. I said bring me the paper, boy . . . the paper *comma*, boy!"

Those who argue against relying too much on the ear say that writing is meant to be seen, not heard, and therefore the eye is more reliable. It's probably unwise to take the extreme of either of these positions.

Whether you are a heavy user or a light user of commas, a little time spent in learning the commonly accepted conventions is time spent in the interest of clear, stylish writing. To illustrate some of the most common punctuation perplexities involving commas, we will offer some groups of sentences and let you decide which of each group is correct. The rule for each example is set in italics below it.

The company's plant, in Florida, employs 600 people.

The company's plant in Florida employs 600 people.

Both sentences are correct, but they differ in meaning. In the first, the commas are needed to set off *in Florida* because the phrase is not essential to the meaning. It simply adds another bit of information. In the second, commas are not used to set off *in Florida,* because the phrase is defining—that is, it tells the reader which plant employs 600 people. The clear implication is that the company has more than one plant.

Here is the rule:

- *Use commas to set off purely descriptive, but not defining, phrases.*

* * *

Congress passed a law prohibiting the sale of ice boxes in Alaska, but the president promptly vetoed the legislation.
Congress passed a law prohibiting the sale of ice boxes in Alaska but the president promptly vetoed the legislation.

The first version is correct.

- *Use a comma before the conjunction in a compound sentence—a sentence composed of two independent clauses, either of which could stand alone.*

Exception: When the clauses are short and the thoughts very closely connected, the comma usually can be omitted:

Congress passed the law but the president vetoed it.

* * *

Congress passed a law prohibiting the sale of ice boxes in Alaska, the President promptly vetoed the legislation.
Congress passed a law prohibiting the sale of ice boxes in Alaska the President promptly vetoed the legislation.

Neither sentence is correct. Obviously, something is needed to separate the clauses, but a comma is not the right tool. A semicolon would work. So would *and* or *but* preceded by a comma. You could also make the two thoughts into separate sentences.

- *Do not use a comma to "splice" two complete thoughts.*

* * *

He opened the door and walked in.
He opened the door, and walked in.

The first is correct. The comma after *door* serves no purpose and should be omitted.

• *Do not use a comma to separate two predicates when they have the same subject.*

* * *

To defend our country is the mission of the armed forces.

To defend our country, is the mission of the armed forces.

The first sentence is the right one.

• *Do not use a comma to separate the subject of a sentence from the predicate.*

* * *

Before she became president of the company, she was sales manager for the Eastern Region.

Before she became president of the company she was sales manager for the Eastern Region.

Either version is acceptable, but we prefer the first.

• *Use a comma after an introductory phrase unless the phrase is very short and there is no chance the sentence will be misread.*

How short is "short"? There is no set length. The writer's ear is probably the best guide to when the comma may be omitted after an introductory phrase. In the following sentence, the comma is required to prevent ambiguity: "Even before she resigned from the company, she founded another company that made similar products." Without the comma after *company*, a reader might be momentarily confused about the relationship of *company* to *founded*. Even though careful reading would make the meaning clear, writers should not burden their readers unnecessarily.

* * *

The Army, Navy, Air Force and Marine Corps participated in the training exercise.

The Army, Navy, Air Force, and Marine Corps participated in the training exercise.

We strongly prefer the second sentence.

• *Use commas to separate items in a series of three or more even if the last item is preceded by* and.

There is a belief in art circles that Rodin's *The Thinker* was trying to remember where he left his pants. We have it on good authority that he was really trying to decide whether to use a comma before *and* in a series. If he had asked the editor of, say, the *New York Times,* he would have gotten no for an answer. But if he had asked the late William Strunk Jr., one of the foremost authorities on English usage, he would have gotten yes.

There is a belief in art circles that Rodin's *The Thinker* was trying to remember where he left his pants. We have it on good authority that he was really trying to decide whether to use a comma before *and* in a series.

There is no consensus on the subject. Many publications do not use the serial comma, but most grammarians and many style manuals, including the respected *Chicago Manual of Style,* recommend it. We contend that the serial comma does no harm but can prevent ambiguity.

Here is what we suggest: Consider the serial comma before *and* to be optional (but preferred) in a short series composed of single words: "The U.S. flag is red, white[,] and blue." Consider it mandatory in (a) a long series, (b) a series composed of more than single words, and (c) any series in which the last two items might be read together, resulting in confusion.

* * *

They live in a large, well-designed, comfortable house.

They live in a large white two-story house.

Both are correct. In the first, the three adjectives describing *house* are of approximately equal importance to the sentence and need to be separated by commas. In the second, the adjectives are so closely related that separation by commas would destroy their effect.

- *Use commas to separate adjectives in a series if they are of equal importance.*

When in doubt, place *and* where the commas would go. If it sounds right, use commas; if not, don't. Notice that "large and well-designed and comfortable" seems to work, but "large and white and two-story" doesn't.

* * *

Miami, Florida, is the home of a large number of Cuban-Americans.

Miami, Florida is the home of a large number of Cuban-Americans.

Choose the first sentence: *Florida* is parenthetical and must be set off by commas.

• *Use a comma after both the city and the state when they appear within a sentence.*

* * *

March 4, 1861, was the day on which Abraham Lincoln was inaugurated.
March 4, 1861 was the day on which Abraham Lincoln was inaugurated.
Abraham Lincoln was inaugurated on 4 March 1861.
Abraham Lincoln was inaugurated on 4 March, 1861.
Abraham Lincoln was inaugurated in March, 1861.
Abraham Lincoln was inaugurated in March 1861.

The first, third, and sixth sentences are correct.

• *Set off the year with commas when a month, day, and year are used in a sentence unless the day precedes the month. Do not use a comma between the month and year when the day of the month is not used.*

* * *

"I'm planning to buy a copy of *Sleeping Dogs Don't Lay* for my illiterate brother-in-law," he said.
"Are you planning to buy a copy of *Sleeping Dogs Don't Lay* for my illiterate brother-in-law?," he asked.

The first sentence is correct. The comma after the question mark in the second is not needed.

• *Use a comma to set off a direct quotation from its attribution* unless *the quotation includes a question mark or an exclamation point.*

* * *

Bill did not accept the job because he wanted more money.
Bill did not accept the job, because he wanted more money.

The first sentence is ambiguous. In the second, the comma after *job* prevents ambiguity. Without it, the reader cannot be sure whether Bill accepted the job. If he did, was it for a reason other than money? If he did not, was it because the job didn't pay enough?

When the order of the clauses is reversed to put the negative after the *because* clause, there is no ambiguity with or without the comma: "Because he wanted to earn more money[,] Bill did not accept the job."

In "Bill accepted the job because he wanted to earn more money," there is no negative statement and therefore no ambiguity.

- *Insert a comma before a* "because" *clause if the clause that precedes it contains a negative statement.*

* * *

The most important "rule" concerning the use of commas is this: *If the addition or omission of a comma makes the meaning clearer, add it or remove it even if doing so seems to violate some other rule.*

IX

Punctuation Perplexities

Punctuation is not just a code of courtesy to readers. Punctuation also affects the *meanings* of messages in crucial ways. Witness this classified ad: "FOR SALE: A quilted high chair that can be made into a table, a pottie chair, a rocking horse, refrigerator, spring coat size 8, and fur collar." That's an amazing high chair! How wonderful that it can be converted to six other objects. A period placed after *table* would have clarified what was being offered.

Read the six sentences below and then punctuate each statement in such a way that its meaning is radically altered.

1. A clever dog knows its master.
2. Call me fool if you wish.
3. Woman without her man is nothing.
4. I saw a man eating lobster.
5. Mary Jane and I went to see the latest Brad Pitt movie.
6. The butler stood at the door and called the guests names.

Now have a look at six apparently confusing sentences. If you provide the proper punctuation, each statement will make complete sense. Answers to these twelve sentences repose in the Answers section at the end of this book.

7. Other than that one thought he was not there.

8. Anne Boleyn kept her head up defiantly an hour after she was beheaded.

9. Every lady in this land
   Hath twenty nails upon each hand
   Five and twenty on hand and feet
   And this is true without deceit.

10. There should be more space between ham and and and and and eggs. (spoken to a sign-painter)

11. That that is is that that is not is not is not that it it is.

12. Mary where John had had had had had had had had had had had the teacher's approval Mary would have been correct.

Full stops

A comma signals a reader to slow down or pause briefly, but a period, colon, dash, or semicolon brings the reader to a full or an almost-full stop. Everyone knows that a period ends a sentence, but the uses of the other stops are less clearly defined. Here are some guidelines:

• **The colon** is next to the period in the strength of the stop. It often introduces quoted matter, a list, or a clause that amplifies the preceding statement:

> To quote Theodore Bernstein in *The Careful Writer:* "The colon heralds fulfillment of a promise implied in what precedes it."

• **The dash** is used to interrupt a sentence and insert parenthetical material. Expressed in words, a dash would be something like "Oh, by the way . . ."

> The English language is often misused by members of the media—the major media are no exceptions—despite the fact that they should set the example for their audiences.

If your keyboard does not have the dash, use two hyphens with no space between them.

• **The semicolon** is used mainly to separate independent clauses that are not linked by a conjunction. Separation of clauses by a semicolon shows a close relationship that might be weakened if the clauses were sentences:

> Margaret was a born leader; she never looked to see if anyone was following.

Semicolons should also be used to separate elements of a series that contains commas:

> The company has offices in San Francisco, California; Atlanta, Georgia; Portland, Oregon; and Vancouver, British Columbia.

The apostrophe

In a recent single-panel cartoon, a young woman is walking by the *Daily News* building. In the window is taped a sign that causes her to do a double take: EDITOR'S WANTED.

That error—using an apostrophe to mark a plural—was intended as a wry comment on the need for editing, and certainly no good editor would allow such an apostrophe catastrophe. Unfortunately, the apostrophe catastrophes that festoon our cartoons are put there without thought.

For example, as the witchy Broom-Hilda approaches the mail box to post her taxes, she starts to shake violently and screams, "Noo! It's my money! Not the governments'! They'll just waste it! Unfair, unfair! Bawwwww!" For another example, Charlie Brown asks a retailer, "Is this where you're selling athlete's autographs?" For a third example, Tank McNamara announces, "The bond election passed. They'll tax themselves $500 million to build a stadium for the Smasher's owner to move there and use rent-free."

Note that the misplacement of the apostrophes in *governments'*, *athlete's*, and *Smasher's* is not perpetrated on purpose.

The apostrophe has four main uses:

1. To show the omission of numbers in such expressions as *Christmas '98* or letters in expressions that imitate certain patterns of speech—*finger lickin' good*.
2. To form contractions (*I'm, we've, can't, they'll*).
3. To form plurals of single numbers and letters: "Mary brought home a report card with two A's and two B's." (The apostrophe is not needed when letters or numbers appear in groups of two or more: *the 1920s, the ABCs, the rule of 78s, two Ph.D.s.*)
4. To form possessives.

The first three uses of the apostrophe are fairly straightforward, but the fourth is widely misunderstood, so let us concentrate on how apostrophes are used to form possessives. That way you won't be dispossessed. Which of the following is correct?

Jones struck it rich by marrying the boss's daughter.
Jones struck it rich by marrying the boss' daughter.

The first is preferred.

• *To form the possessive of a singular noun, add an apostrophe and an* s, *even if the noun ends in* s.

Sounds simple, but maybe it isn't. Complications arise when a singular word ends in a sibilant, which is a sort of hissing sound (*s*, *z*, *c*, or *x*). Some publications have adopted the practice of adding only the apostrophe to such words. For example, the possessive of *boss*, according to that practice, is *boss'*. This results in such sentences as "He married the boss' daughter," which is offensive to our ears and incorrect according to most grammarians. Some publications that have adopted that style insist that possessives of such proper names as *Gomez* and *Lomax* be formed in the same way. Thus, in these publications, the possessive of *Gomez* is rendered as *Gomez'* and the possessive of *Lomax* as *Lomax'*.

According to the rule cited at the beginning of this discussion, possessives of those three words should be *boss's*, *Gomez's*, and *Lomax's*. In all three, the appended *s* is pronounced. Therefore, logic is on the side of the rule.

Some exceptions are allowed by authorities who accept the rule as we have stated it. *The Chicago Manual of Style* allows exceptions when "tradition and euphony dictate the use of the apostrophe only." It does not make an exception for proper names that end in *s*. Strunk and White suggest adding the apostrophe without the *s* to form the possessives of ancient proper names such as *Moses* and *Achilles*. *The New York Times Stylebook* permits dropping the final *s* when including it would result in two or more sibilants preceding the apostrophe, as in *Kansas' governor,* or when a word beginning with a sibilant follows, as in *for appearance' sake*.

* * *

We're playing bridge tonight at the Jones's house.
We're playing bridge tonight at the Jones' house.
We're playing bridge tonight at the Joneses' house.

The third sentence is the only correct one.

• *To form the possessive of a plural noun, add an apostrophe only, except for nouns such as* men *and* people *that have irregular plurals and are treated as if they were singular when the possessives are formed.*

The plural of *Jones* is *Joneses.*

Back in the fall of 1996, one of your user-friendly authors drove up and down Route 93 in Boston past a multiplex cinema. On the prominent marquee of the theater, emblazoned with the titles of a dozen films, he noted, week after week, FIRST WIVE'S CLUB.

As time passed, he expected that surely somebody would correct the atrocity, but nooooo—it stayed there. Apparently the sign supervisor and the bevy of others associated with running the theater believed that Bette Midler, Diane Keaton, and Goldie Hawn were each a "wive."

The primary example of apostrophe catastrophe these days is the word *kids*. In fact, we challenge you, O verbivorous reader, to find one example in which *kids* in the possessive is cobbled correctly.

Boston Market advertises "New! Kid's Meal. Starting at $1.99." So one kid walks into the restaurant and the place has to close because the staff has met its quota for the day!

On a tube of Crest toothpaste is printed the label "Kid's Sparkle Fun Gel."

Gold's Gym announces "J. W. Tumbles, A Kid's Gym. Featuring: Kid's Fitness programs & Kid's Swim Lessons."

Please aid the cause of literacy in our punctuationally challenged nation: When more than one child is involved, the possessive is not *kid's* It's *kids'*. We kid you not.

* * *

It is really pleasant to take one's time when playing golf.

It is really pleasant to take ones time when playing golf.

This house is our's.

This house is ours.

Sentences one and four are correct.

• *Do not use an apostrophe to form the possessive of personal pronouns, except for the pronoun* one.

* * *

Let's all ride in John's and Pedro's car.

Let's all ride in John and Pedro's car.

The second sentence is correct. The context shows that only one car is discussed. *John's and Pedro's car* implies two cars. The phrase is elliptical for *John's car and Pedro's car*. *John's and Pedro's cars* would be ambiguous because the reader would be unable to determine whether John and Pedro had more than one car each.

• *When two or more words, taken as a unit, show joint possession, use the possessive form with the last only.*

The hyphen

We recently spotted a sign that read, TWO ACRE LOTS FOR SALE. What did the sign really say? What did it offer for sale? We asked several people. Most said it offered an unspecified number of two-acre lots. One person, however, thought it offered two one-acre lots for sale.

We recently spotted a sign that read, TWO ACRE LOTS FOR SALE.

Even if only one person misunderstood, the sign failed to communicate an unambiguous message. Maybe the person who misunderstood was in the market for a two-acre lot and didn't bother to answer the ad because it seemed to offer one-acre lots. A simple hyphen would have prevented any possibility of ambiguity: "two-acre lots for sale."

In one notorious case, the omission of a hyphen resulted in a business loss. A supervisor wrote, "I need the six foot long rods by Friday." What he needed was six-foot-long rods, not the six foot-long rods he received. The ambiguity cost the firm $25,000.

The main purpose of the hyphen is to prevent awkward or confusing constructions. Most often, hyphens join two or more words that, taken together, form an adjective. Examples: *business-writing seminar, front-office decision, in-house legal counsel, state-of-the-art equipment.* In such examples, the hyphens ensure clarity and make reading easier. Use of hyphens in this way has been hotly debated by writers. Some favor hyphens in all such constructions. Others use hyphens when they are necessary to prevent ambiguity.

Some additional uses for hyphens are as follows:

• To avoid awkward double- or triple-letter combinations. Examples: *re-elect, anti-industrial, pre-eminent.*

• To form compound numbers less than one hundred, such as *twenty-one, sixty-seven, ninety-nine, three-sixteenths, one-fourth.*

• To join a prefix to a proper noun, as in *un-American, pre-Christmas, ex-president Carter, anti-Communist.* Do not use a hyphen to join an adverb that ends in *ly* with another word to form a compound. No hyphens are needed in *publicly held company, wholly owned subsidiary, widely known facts.*

Parentheses

There's not much debate about the use of parentheses, but they are often used when commas or dashes would serve as well and would be less distracting. Some manuals say that material in parentheses carries less emphasis than material set off by commas or dashes. But that distinction is a fine one at best. When the material to be enclosed is a complete sentence, the punctuation is within the parentheses.

Parentheses should always be in pairs. Some publications use a single parenthesis with numbers or letters marking items in a series:

> The plaintiff asked for a) restitution for damages b) attorney's fees c) written assurance that similar incidents would not occur again.

If there's a reason for not using pairs of parentheses to enclose *a, b,* and *c,* we're not aware of it.

Question mark

When a sentence ends with a quoted question, the question mark is the terminal punctuation, and a period is not needed:

> Turning to face the president, the reporter asked, "Mr. President, what is your reaction to the trade bill now being debated in Congress?"

When a sentence begins with a quoted question, the question mark eliminates the need for a comma to set off the quotation from the attribution:

> "What is your opinion of the bill now being debated in Congress?" the reporter asked the president.

Question marks are used only with direct questions, not when questions are simply referred to. Examples:

> In the Watergate hearings, Senator Baker asked the now-famous question, what did the president know and when did he know it.
>
> The now-famous question, what did the president know and when did he know it, was asked by Senator Baker in the Watergate hearings.

Quotation marks

The main uses of quotation marks are to set off direct quotations, titles of short works, words or phrases used in an unusual way, and nicknames. With direct quotations, confusion persists about the placement of punctuation in relation to the quotation marks. The conventions are not all logical, but here they are:

- Periods and commas always go inside the quotation marks:

> "The company is in good financial shape," he said.
>
> He said, "The company is in good financial shape."

- Semicolons always go outside the quotation marks:

> He said, "The company is in good financial shape"; then he proceeded to cite figures that led to a different conclusion.

• Question marks and exclamation marks go either inside or outside, depending on whether the question or exclamation is part of the quoted material:

Mr. Jones asked, "What is the source of that information?"
Was it Mr. Jones who sighed, "I can't stand the heat in this kitchen"?

• A quotation within a quotation is set off by single quotation marks:

"One of my favorite lines," he said, "is Dylan Thomas's 'Do not go gentle into that good night.' "

Note that both the single and double quotation marks go after the period.

In most of the United Kingdom, these conventions are slightly different. Commas are always placed outside the quotation marks; but periods, question marks, and exclamation points are placed either inside or outside as the sense of the sentence dictates.

• Short works whose titles are set off by quotation marks include poems, book chapters, magazine articles, songs, and short stories. Longer works, such as motion pictures, books, operas, and concertos, usually appear in italics. Italics are indicated in typewritten copy by underlining.

• A word or phrase used in an unusual way is enclosed in quotation marks the first time it is so used. Unless there is a lot of space between the first and subsequent uses, the quotation marks are necessary only once.

Exclamation point

Exclamation points are beloved of high school sophomores, but professional writers use them sparingly. An exclamation point is a poor substitute for a well-constructed sentence. Never use more than one!!!

Ellipsis points

When something is omitted from quoted material, three spaced periods (. . .) are used to indicate the omission. These are called ellipsis points. For spacing purposes, they are treated as a three-letter word:

> "We the people of the United States . . . do ordain and establish this Constitution. . . ."

In that abbreviation of the preamble to the United States Constitution, words are omitted in two places. Note that three dots are used to show the first omission but four are used for the second. When the material preceding the omission ("We the people of the United States") is a sentence fragment, only three dots are needed. When the preceding material can stand alone as a sentence, as in the case with the shortened preamble, four are required. The first dot represents a sentence-ending period; the three others are the ellipsis points indicating the omission. If the sentence is a question or an exclamation, a question mark or an exclamation point is followed by three ellipsis points.

Style manuals differ on ellipsis points. Some simplify the matter by suggesting three dots (. . .) for an omission, no matter where it occurs. Others, especially manuals for preparation of academic manuscripts, have stringent rules. We suggest that you adopt a style that suits you and use it consistently.

X

A Ten-Minute Writing Lesson

Most Americans over the age of fifty remember a magazine advertisement with the heading, "They laughed when I sat down to play." The ad copy waxed enthusiastic about some quick and easy system for learning to play piano. We won't say it didn't work; we never tried it. But the people we know who play piano with great proficiency have worked hard to learn how and continue to labor mightily to improve.

The same can be said for writing: People who write well have spent many years learning the craft, and there is always something new to master. If there is a quick and easy way, we wish we had found it a long time ago.

What you are about to read comprises ten of the most important principles of writing that we have learned over the years. We present them first in a concise form that enables you to assimilate them in about a minute each. Then we provide some examples and elaboration to strengthen your understanding. After that it is up to you to commit the time and effort to put them into practice in your own writing.

We are basing this discussion on three premises:

1. Everyone ought to write better, and anyone can learn to write better.
2. The fundamentals of good writing apply to all kinds of writing, although some special kinds of writing, such as poetry, have special rules.
3. Good writing is writing that does what it is supposed to do—that is, it causes the reader to think, feel, or act as the writer wishes.

Clarity is both the indispensable ingredient and the inevitable result of good writing. W. Somerset Maugham wrote: "Anything is better than not to write clearly. There is nothing to be said against lucidity, and against simplicity only the possibility of dryness. This is a risk well worth taking when you reflect how much better it is to be bald than to wear a curly wig."

This ten-minute writing lesson is not going to give you a magic formula that will make you a better writer. It is not going to turn you into an instant journalist or enable you to write that novel you've had sloshing around in your mind all these years. And it is not going to stop your friends from laughing when you sit down at your computer or typewriter.

Having provided the necessary caveats, let us tell you what this lesson can do:

Build your confidence.

Time and time again in writing seminars we have conducted, participants have told us that the most important thing they gained from the seminar was the knowledge that they could improve their writing. Many people have the right instincts, but their sense of what makes good writing might have been dulled by exposure to the garbage that passes for writing these days. In a business-writing seminar, a young woman expressed surprise at the seminar leader's suggestion to choose *use* instead of *utilize* in an exercise emphasizing simple language. Why the surprise? "My boss, who is a very smart man, always changes *use* to *utilize* in anything I write," she explained. The seminar leader assured her that it was okay to use *use* instead of utilizing *utilize*. Her confidence was restored.

Review principles.

Many of us learned a lot about writing well when we were students but allowed the skill to deteriorate. We predict that when you read some of our principles you'll say, "Yes, I knew that," or "Of course, that makes sense." You will be pleased to find that some of the principles overlap, or one may depend on another. For example, when you choose the active voice rather than the passive and avoid nominalizing verbs, as we discuss in the Third Principle, you automatically use fewer words, as we advocate in the First Principle.

Provide a foundation.

Whenever you set out to do something—whether it's building a house, painting a picture, or learning to write better—a good foundation is essential. The principles we will discuss can be the foundation on which you build your skill as a writer.

Gain a new perspective on writing.

If this discussion does nothing else, it will give you a new way to look at writing. It will illustrate how certain habits, good and bad, affect writing. It will make you more critical—critical in the positive sense—of what you read and help you to understand what makes good writing good and bad writing bad.

Perhaps most important, it will sharpen your ability to recognize and correct your own faults. Jacques Barzun, the distinguished writer and educator, wrote in *Simple & Direct:* "The whole world will tell you, if you care to ask, that your words should be simple and direct. Everybody likes the other fellow's words *plain*."

The trick is to write the way you'd like for others to write.

Here are the ten principles in capsule form.

- **Cut the Verbal Clutter.** *Train yourself to write with fewer words. Your readers will love you for it. If you can make twenty-five words do the work of fifty, you have reduced by half the amount of material the reader must assimilate to get the intended message.*
- **Keep it Simple.** *Contrary to what some people seem to believe, simple writing is not the product of simple minds. A simple, unpretentious style has both grace and power. By not calling attention to itself it allows the reader to focus on the message.*
- **Power Up with Verbs.** *The source of all energy, strength, and motion in a sentence is the verb. How well you use verbs determines to a large extent how persuasively you write.*

Power up with verbs.

• **Don't Overstuff Your Sentences.** *As a* general *rule, a sentence should have no more than one main idea. We emphasize* general *because this rule, like so many others, is violated by some good writers.*

• **Don't "Adjectivize" Nouns.** *Next to verbs, nouns are the most important part of speech. Like verbs, they are weakened when the writer tries to turn them into something they are not.*

• **Use Modifiers Sparingly.** *The writer who chooses strong, active verbs and vivid, colorful nouns has less need for adverbs and adjectives. Carefully chosen and sparingly used, adjectives and adverbs can serve a writer well. But they should be considered guilty until proven innocent—guilty of making writing fat and sluggish.*

• **Set Your Work in Concrete.** *If the purpose of writing is to convey ideas and information, then unnecessary or unintended abstraction defeats the purpose. The more concrete the writing, the more precise the message it conveys.*

• **Watch Your Language.** *Words mean things. You can no more write well without using words well than a composer can create a symphony without understanding rhythm and harmony. Good writers know that connotations are often more important than definitions,* *and that the true meaning of a word or phrase is the effect it has on readers.*

• **Help the Reader.** *An often-repeated axiom is that communication is a two-way street. But clear communication is the responsibility of the writer, not the reader. The writer must therefore give the reader all possible help in understanding what is written.*

• **Train the Ear.** *Writing is at once a visual and an aural medium. Although not all writing is intended to be read aloud, most good writing* can *be read aloud with no detrimental effect. It is important, therefore, for anyone who wants to write well to train the ear to recognize the good and bad aural qualities.*

Now let's examine each principle in more detail:

The First Principle: Cut the verbal clutter.

Train yourself to write with fewer words. Your readers will love you for it. If you can make twenty-five words do the work of fifty, you have reduced by half the amount of material the reader must assimilate to get the intended message.

If we were writing commandments instead of principles of good writing, this would have to be the first and greatest. Fat writing, which is to say writing cluttered with unnecessary words, is surely the cause of more bad writing than any other fault. Again quoting Barzun, "Communication is most complete when it proceeds from the smallest number of words—and indeed of syllables." Consider, for example, this sentence, which we encountered in a brochure touting a business-writing seminar offered by a large national concern: "There is no easy shortcut to expressing yourself well by means of the written word." Evidently, the copy writer had not taken the course. Why not "There is no shortcut to good writing"?

Take a sample of writing, yours or someone else's, and remove every word that does not contribute to the meaning. You will be amazed at how many words are unnecessary. You might become addicted to fat-cutting.

One reason for writing with fewer words is that good ideas can be lost in a sea of verbiage. The fewer the words, the more memorable the message. An executive wrote, in a message to employees: "We are already a world-class organization in many ways. Our goal now is to build, through effective consultation with our customers and aggressive response to our mutually beneficial aims, a sustained reputation as world class in the area of customer satisfaction."

The simple, but important, idea is almost choked to death. Our revision would be something like this: "We are already a world-class organization in almost every way. Our goal now is to build a world-class sales organization." The force of thought is preserved in half the number of words.

Several years ago a full-page ad appeared in the *Wall Street Journal* as "An Open Letter to President and Mrs. Clinton on Containing Health Care Costs." It contained this bloated sentence:

> If we are to truly rein in health care costs' explosive growth, it is imperative that your upcoming health care program recognize and incent the use of technologies and medical instrumentation that cut costs, and that the program does not shortsightedly cap the purchase of instrumentation or technology that may cost more up front, but can result in significant reductions in the overall cost of treating patients.

Let's analyze the sentence:

> If we are to truly [unnecessary] rein in *[stop]* health care costs' [the possessive *health care costs'* is awkward] explosive growth, it is imperative that [*we must* is both shorter and more forceful] your upcoming [unnecessary] health care program recognize and incent [a nonword] the use of technologies and medical instrumentation [*technologies* should be sufficient] that cut costs, and that the program does not shortsightedly [*shortsighted*

is an important point, but using its adverbial form weakens it] cap the purchase of instrumentation or technology [repetitive] that may cost more up front, but can result in significant reductions [the simpler and shorter "cost a lot less" would be better] the overall [unnecessary] cost of treating patients [unnecessary; who else would be treated?].

We would revise the sentence as follows:

If your program is to stop the growth of health care costs, it must provide incentives for the use of cost-cutting medical technologies. To cap the purchase of such technologies would be shortsighted. They might cost more initially, but they can reduce treatment costs significantly.

None of this should be construed to mean that our writing should be like the old Dick and Jane children's book: "See Jane. See Dick. See Dick chase Jane." It simply means that every word in a sentence must have a reason to be there. A word that seems to add nothing to meaning might be defensible for emphasis, balance, transition, or rhythm. Someone asked a well-known author why he had chosen two words instead of a single word that expressed the meaning. He answered, "I needed another syllable." We've no doubt that his reason was legitimate. But most writers, most of the time, ought to take the attitude that if two words are good, one word is twice as good.

Author Sydney Smith offered this formula for achieving conciseness: "In composing, as a general rule, run your pen through every other word you have written; you have no idea what vigor it will give to your style."

The Second Principle: Keep it simple.

Contrary to what some people seem to believe, simple writing is not the product of simple minds. A simple, unpretentious style has both grace and power. By not calling attention to itself it allows the reader to focus on the message.

A freelance writer advertising for clients describes herself as "a simplifier." Her ad copy explains that she specializes in writing simply about complex subjects.

The ability to simplify complex subjects is a skill to be prized. Imagine how much easier life would be if manuals for computer software, instructions for assembling children's toys, and explanations of tax laws were written by "simplifiers." Unfortunately, software manuals seem to be written by people whose first language is COBOL, toy-instruction sheets by mechanical engineers who are idiots savants, and tax documents by, well, who knows?

Inept writers are more likely to be "desimplifiers"—writers who make something seem more complicated than it is. The manager of a large industrial plant bought a series of videotapes designed to help parents cope with problems of teenagers and made the tapes available to employees. In announcing the availability of the tapes, the manager wrote:

> Research and available data about employee performance indicates that there is a relationship between an employee's frame of mind and safe work behavior. It is now more fully recognized that if an employee has personal and family problems on his or her mind, their ability to concentrate on their work can be impacted. One area that is particularly distractful [sic] to employees is erratic or unusual behavior of children, especially teenaged youngsters.

Ignoring the errors in grammar, word use, and punctuation, we cite this as an example of a simple idea made complicated by overblown prose, fuzzy concepts, and excess words. The whole idea is to make employees safer. Phrases such as "relationship between an employee's frame of mind," "safe work behavior," "more fully recognized," and "can be impacted" are vague at best.

The entire paragraph can be expressed in fewer than half the words: "Research has shown that workers with personal problems are more likely to have accidents. This is especially true when a problem involves the employee's teenage child."

Sometimes an inappropriate analogy gets in the way of clear understanding. A large investment company told clients, in an "Investment Opportunities" bulletin:

> Just as in skiing, you get the best performance when you keep your upper body facing the direction you want to go and turn your lower body from side to side to maneuver the smooth or bumpy hill; investors must continue to focus on their primary investment objectives and make appropriate steps to maneuver in the recent tough market.

An analogy is supposed to clarify. In the example above, the message is subordinate to the skiing lesson.

An art studio, seeking a gallery to handle its work, sent prospects a message beginning with this largely meaningless, jargon-clogged paragraph:

> We are looking for a gallery that is used to working with new conceptualizations in art momentum. We are working with the combinational theories of art processed as a state of being. Through this we create art that coordinates the process of molecular awareness with the concept of reason and scale perception. This we refer to as imprintsial patterns. These patterns are expressed in art form to enable their sectional circumference to be photographed by the lens of the eye. This is a very accelerated mode of transport of harmonial movement that balances the personal requirement for centeredness. We expect to find

> many means of expressing these concepts and art is one mode of expressed beingness that we wish to see.

Reading that—it's real, folks; we didn't make it up—we get the distinct feeling that someone is tugging on our leg. We wonder how van Gogh, Rodin, Rembrandt, or Grandma Moses would react to such garbage. The writer seems more concerned about impressing than communicating an honest message.

Good writers are not afraid to use short, everyday words. They know it's possible to write clearly, convincingly, and even powerfully with short words. An item titled "The Long and Short of It," from the Members' Handbook of the Society for the Preservation of English Language and Literature, illustrates:

> You don't have to use long words when you write. Most of the time, you can make your points quite well with short ones. In fact, big words may get in the way of what you want to say. And what's more, when you write with short words, no one will need to look them up to learn what they mean.
>
> Short words can make us feel good. They can run and jump and dance and soar high in the clouds. They can kill the chill of a cold night and help us keep cool on a hot day. They fill our hearts with joy, but they can bring tears to our eyes, too. A short word can be soft or strong. It can sting like a bee or sing like a lark. Small words of love can move us, charm us, lull us to sleep. Short words give us light and hope and peace and love and health and a lot more good things. A small word can be as sweet as the taste of a ripe pear, or tart like plum jam.
>
> Small words help us to think. They are, in truth, the heart and the soul of clear thought.
>
> When you write, choose the short word if you can find one that will let you say what you want to say. If there is no short

one that fills the bill, then go ahead and consider the utilization of a sesquipedalian expression as a viable alternative, but be cognizant of the actuality that it could conceivably be incumbent upon many of your perusers to expend, by consulting a dictionary or perhaps an alternate lexicon of particularized patois, copious amounts of their invaluable time in attempting to determine the message you are endeavoring to impart to them through the instrumentality of your missive.

Note that *ahead,* in the second sentence of the last paragraph, is the first word of more than one syllable.

Remember, you do not have to use big words to express big ideas. If you doubt this, consider the words that Winston Churchill, Abraham Lincoln, and Thomas Jefferson used to express some of their most profound ideas. Read the Declaration of Independence and the preamble to the Constitution. Review the speeches of John Kennedy, Martin Luther King Jr., Ronald Reagan, and General Douglas MacArthur. Rediscover the beauty and simplicity of the King James Bible.

The Third Principle: Power up with verbs.

The source of all energy, strength, and motion in a sentence is the verb. How well you use verbs determines to a large extent how persuasively you write.

We love the Energizer commercials that show the bunny marching on while other toys, presumably with inferior batteries, are faltering. Sentences are like that. A sentence with a weak verb grinds along like a toy with a weak battery. The writer who chooses verbs wisely and uses them well produces copy that, like the Energizer bunny, keeps going . . . and going.

To help you power up your sentences by choosing and using verbs more effectively, we offer these suggestions:

1. Choose the active voice rather than the passive unless you have a good reason to choose the passive. In other words, make the active voice the voice of choice most of the time.

2. Look for alternatives to the verb *to be,* in all its forms—*is, am, are, were, was,* et al.

3. Don't hesitate to use strong, gutsy verbs.

4. Don't nominalize verbs.

Active vs. passive voice

In our discussion of writing and usage myths ("Things You *Know* That Just Ain't So"), we defended the passive voice because we feel that some writing teachers have unjustly maligned that often useful, sometimes necessary, construction. Having done our duty to the downtrodden, we now turn to the more energetic active.

Read the following and see whether it strikes a familiar chord:

> And all this would come about because two men had been accurately judged by Seab Cooley: James Morton, who was hardly known by Cooley at all, and Brigham Anderson, who was known by Cooley quite well and had been studied by him with considerable care. Cooley had been told by his instinct that the man who was known by Washington under his right name would be crumbled when suddenly presented with the ghost of James Morton from the past; and he had been told by his instinct that Senator Anderson, confronted with equal suddenness with the same knowledge, would act as directly and forcefully as he had.

You might have remembered the names of the characters in Allen Drury's novel, *Advise & Consent,* but you would not have recognized the passage from the writing style. We paraphrased it by converting Drury's active sentences to passive. Our version contains 106 words. Compare it with the ninety-six-word original:

> And all of this would come about because Seab Cooley had accurately judged two men: James Morton, whom he hardly knew at all, and Brigham Anderson, whom he knew quite well and had studied with considerable care. His instinct had told him that the man Washington knew under his right name would crumble when suddenly presented with the ghost of James Morton from the past; and his instinct had told him that Senator Anderson, confronted with equal suddenness with the same knowledge, would act as directly and forcefully as he had.

The word-count difference is small, but the original is a smoother, more engaging, less sluggish paragraph. Consider another example, paraphrased from *Reinventing the Corporation,* by John Naisbitt and Patricia Aburdene, with a greater difference in word count:

> More than 60 percent of the money spent by corporations on health care for employees is paid to hospitals. So when minor surgery is needed by an employee, money can be saved by the company if the employee is sent elsewhere for the surgery to be performed.

Our paraphrase contains forty-seven words; the original, twenty-nine:

> More than 60 percent of corporate health care costs go toward hospital bills. So when people need minor surgery, it makes sense to consider doing it outside a hospital.

One reason that active-voice sentences are livelier is that the active voice must always have an agent—or doer—expressed. That is the essence of action. That's why some have labeled the passive "the nobody voice."

To be or not to be

It is impossible to write without using forms of *to be,* and we don't advocate that you try. We do suggest that you examine what you have written and look for ways to replace *to be* with stronger verbs. Consider, for example, the third-to-last sentence in the previous section: "One reason that active-voice sentences are . . ." We might have written, as an alternative: "Active-voice sentences make livelier prose because . . ." In that example, eliminating *are* and *is* means recasting the sentence, but the result is a stronger sentence.

A writer who must create edge-of-the-seat excitement will always seek vivid, action-packed verbs over bland *to be* verbs, as this passage from *Fighting Fire,* by Caroline Paul, illustrates:

> Simultaneously Williams reaches and jumps at a fence that lines the other side of the yard. I grab a foot and a knee and push him up. He teeters at the top and then shimmies to a small roof next to the burning building. I grab a chain saw and pass it to him.

Nine verbs and not a *be* in the bunch.

Eliminating *to be* is difficult. You need not institute a full-court press to do so, but make yourself aware of how overuse of those verb forms can rob prose of energy.

Gutsy verbs

Basically, English verbs come in two varieties—short, "everyday" verbs, often of Anglo-Saxon origin, and Latinate verbs that tend to be longer and are usually more formal. We think of the former as gutsy verbs.

Gutsy verbs are often about people; they have life. They *are* life. You cannot write them or read them without envisioning real, live, flesh-and-blood people engaged in live, flesh-and-blood actions. Here are some gutsy verbs with their more formal counterparts:

make	*fabricate*	*show*	*exhibit*
give	*donate*	*claim*	*postulate*
free	*extricate*	*tell*	*relate*
think	*cogitate*	*help*	*assist*
use	*utilize*	*see*	*observe*
die	*expire*	*act (for)*	*represent*
happen	*transpire*	*teach*	*instruct*

We do not say that using more formal words is wrong or makes writing bad. But for sheer energy, *make* beats *fabricate* any old day. And we'd much rather free you than extricate you from the burden of having to use long, formal words.

Nominalizing verbs

Writers who prefer long, formal words to the gutsy words described above love to turn perfectly good verbs into nouns. This process is called nominalization. *Decide* becomes *decision*, and requires two more words to say the same thing: "Make a decision."

Verb-to-noun conversions rob prose of vitality. *Take action, bring to a conclusion, find a solution, make a determination, reach an agreement, make an error, turn a profit, draw to a close, give a performance,* and *file a lawsuit* are the same as *act, conclude, solve, determine, agree, err, profit, close, perform,* and *sue.*

When you revise, be alert for nominalizations and convert them back into verbs. It can do wonders for your writing.

The Fourth Principle: Don't overstuff your sentences.

As a general rule, a sentence should have no more than one main idea. We emphasize general *because this rule, like so many others, is violated by some good writers.*

Packing too much into a sentence makes it doubly hard to keep the elements in the proper relationship to each other. Research described by Theodore Bernstein in *Watch Your Language* showed in sample texts a correlation between average sentence length and comprehensibility—the shorter each sentence, the better the reader's comprehension. This led to Bernstein's advocacy of "one sentence, one idea."

An article in the *New York Times,* America's standard-setting newspaper, included this sentence:

> As of early evening, after the president had had two sets of meetings with Vice President Al Gore, Leon Panetta, who is stepping down as White House chief of staff, and his successor, Erskine Bowles, sandwiched around a round of golf, the White House press secretary Michael McCurry said Clinton had not settled on a team.

This fifty-six-word sentence mentions five names and includes at least six items of information that the reader has to process to get to the essential message. Forty-six words separate the *when* ("as of early evening") from the *what* ("Clinton had not settled on a team"). We must also question the meaning of "two sets of meetings." How many meetings compose a "set"? We won't bother to comment on the dissonant and illogical phrase, "sandwiched around a round."

Here is one possible revision:

> As of early evening, said White House press secretary Mike McCurry, President Clinton had not settled on a team. During the day the president had had meetings with Vice President Al Gore; Leon Panetta, who is stepping down as chief of staff; and Panetta's successor, Erskine Bowles. The president sandwiched a round of golf between meetings.

A book review in the *Atlanta Constitution* included this unwieldy sentence:

> While the [*New York*] *Times* became evermore solid, largely through the wise reinvestment of its profits, the *Herald-Tribune*, first under Helen's older son, Whitie, who was signally lacking in leadership ability, and then her brash, energetic, overbearing second son Brown, floundered embarrassingly through a succession of meager efforts, such as a doomed Early Bird edition, and a beneath-its-dignity puzzle contest called Tangle Towns, to save the paper.

Quickly, now: What does the sentence say? What does "to save the paper" refer to? How many different items of information are packed into the sentence?

Our revision eliminates some of the modifiers and breaks the long sentence into three shorter sentences, each with one basic thought:

> While the *Times* became more solid largely through reinvestment of its profits, the *Herald-Tribune* floundered, first under Helen's older son, Whitie, then under her second son, Brown. Whitie lacked leadership ability; Brown was energetic but overbearing. Their meager efforts to save the paper included a doomed Early Bird edition and a beneath-its-dignity puzzle called Tangle Towns.

The Fifth Principle: Don't "adjectivize" nouns.

Next to verbs, nouns are the most important part of speech. Like verbs, they are weakened when the writer tries to turn them into something they are not.

Men and women who work with tools know what can happen when a tool is used to do a job it wasn't designed to do: The job might be botched and the tool damaged. Good writers know that each part of speech has a purpose. When a writer forces one part of speech to do the work of another, the results likely will be unsatisfactory.

We have discussed the practice of converting verbs to nouns, which wastes words and weakens sentences. An equally lamentable practice is converting nouns into adjectives. Weather forecasters, it seems, prefer "shower activity" to old-fashioned showers or simple rain. Crises seem to be obsolete, but "crisis situations" abound. And who wants to face up to the fact that the city has slums when "slum areas" are so much easier to accept?

These and other examples of nouns modifying other nouns are especially common in business writing. Lawyers and engineers are fond of adjectivizing nouns. Writers of business documents often adopt the practice to give their writing a pseudotechnical or pseudolegal cast.

An article on suburban development points out, "The utilities and transportation infrastructure have not kept pace with commercial development." Aside from the fact that the singular subject, *infrastructure,* requires the verb *has,* the sentence complicates a simple concept by using *infrastructure,* which requires adjectivized nouns to explain what it means. "Utilities and transportation" is less burdensome to the reader than "utilities and transportation infrastructure."

Ronald Goldfarb and James C. Raymond, in *Clear Understandings,* an excellent guide to legal writing, deplore the practice of converting nouns into adjectives. They deplore especially "noun chains"—strings of nouns modifying each other. Goldfarb and Raymond call noun chains "ugly and pretentious," and point out that noun chains place an unnecessary burden on a reader.

If you want to find examples of noun chains, corporate financial communications are a likely source. The quarterly report of an oil company is replete with such clumsy phrases as "oil and gas liquids sales," "oil and gas exploration costs," and "products profit margins." Another company's quarterly report laments the "United States sales representative recruiting difficulty." Still another tells its shareholders that the chief executive has appointed "an automation hardware selection team."

Constructing noun chains is sometimes defended as a way to save words; and it is true that all but one of the examples cited above require fewer words than their alternatives. (Example: "costs of exploring for oil and gas" instead of "oil and gas exploration costs.") But the saving of words in these cases is false economy. Its cost is clarity and grace. Although most good writers are word misers, none will hesitate to use an extra word or two when doing so will make a sentence clearer or more natural. "Oil and gas exploration costs" has only five words; "costs of exploring for oil and gas" has seven. Even though the alternative is slightly longer, it *seems* shorter and is much easier to read. That's because a reader of the original must redefine the adjectivized nouns to discern their meaning in context.

Turning nouns into adjectives doesn't violate any rule. In fact, it is standard in phrases like *schoolchildren, kitchen cabinet,* and *government official*. But those expressions serve a purpose. "Oil and gas exploration costs" does not.

The Sixth Principle: Use modifiers sparingly.

The writer who chooses strong, active verbs and vivid, colorful nouns has less need for adverbs and adjectives. Carefully chosen and sparingly used, adjectives and adverbs can serve a writer well. But they should be considered guilty until proven innocent—guilty of making writing fat and sluggish.

Modifiers—adverbs and adjectives—are among the writer's important tools. Used with discretion, they add strength and interest. Used thoughtlessly or excessively, they add nothing but flab. Too many modifiers are cloying, like too much blue cheese on your salad.

Here, for example, is a sentence from a music review published in the *Atlanta Constitution:* "Tubin's music was pleasantly ethnic, rhythmically danceable, modestly inspired, and imaginably appropriate in context."

We're not music critics, but "rhythmically danceable," "modestly inspired," and "imaginably appropriate" strike us as too many beats to the measure.

A product designed to help smokers curb the desire for nicotine advertises that it offers "the power to quit—successfully." Quit *successfully*? A smoker either quits or not. Convert the phrase to a negative and hear how absurd it sounds: "the power not to quit . . . unsuccessfully." Omitting *successfully* would strengthen the sentence because the strong verb *quit* would be a powerful ending. The adverb *successfully* makes a weak sentence-ender.

A news release from a large Southern university, a school with high standards, reports, "The ensemble concertizes constantly throughout [the state] and performs informative concerts to thousands of schoolchildren." Even if we could accept the invented verb, *concertize,* which we are informed is common among musicians, we question whether *constantly* and *informative* add to the thought. The sentence is fat. What's wrong with "The ensemble performs for schoolchildren throughout [the state]"? The release goes on to describe the ensemble's artistic director as "an *active* composer-performer" (our emphasis). Is it possible to be an *inactive* composer-performer? Well, maybe. If such was the point, and if it was worth making, it was worth a few words of explanation.

Many adjectives and adverbs can be omitted without sacrificing anything important. And when they can be, they should be. Words such as *constantly, informative,* and *active,* as they are used in the example, may be evidence of a writer's lack of confidence in strong, simple words. Well-chosen nouns and verbs rarely need the intensification adjectives and adverbs are supposed to provide. *Perform,* for example, evokes an active image, but *concertize* tiptoes around the subject and seems to require *constantly* to make its point.

Adverbs contribute more to bloated prose than adjectives do. Writers who are uncomfortable with simple, direct expression love for something to be done successfully, effectively, actually, or totally. Often these adverbs—and slightly less often their adjectival forms—are redundant. Expressions such as "blared loudly" and "willingly agreed" are so common they scarcely elicit a chuckle. They deserve a hoot.

Knowing the value of understatement and harboring a distaste for overstatement, good writers seldom use such gushy superlatives as *terrific, wonderful, marvelous,* and *fantastic.* They prefer to give facts and let the reader supply the adjectives. Besides, conversational overuse of those words and their likes has rendered them all but meaningless.

"As to the adjective," Mark Twain wrote, "when in doubt, strike it out." Author Marcia Davenport was equally antagonistic toward adverbs: "A really civilized and cultivated writer of the English language will turn inside out to avoid adverbs."

Some words usually cannot be modified without creating a redundancy. Nevertheless, writers addicted to fat can't seem to resist the temptation to add a modifier where none is needed. *Unique,* for example, is seen often with a useless appendage such as *very, totally,* or *somewhat. Unique* means "one of a kind." Nothing can be more unique or less unique.

Could is another example. *Could* should never be accompanied by *possibly. Perfect* means perfect, and that's as far as you can go. Much as we admire the Constitution of the United States, we would prefer that it had been ordained to form "a perfect union" or "a stronger union" rather than "a *more* perfect union." All things considered, we can forgive the framers of that magnificent document for one redundancy.

The Seventh Principle: Set your work in concrete.

If the purpose of writing is to convey ideas and information, then unnecessary or unintended abstraction defeats the purpose. The more concrete the writing, the more precise the message it conveys.

Good writers prefer concrete language to abstract. If you write, for example, that several members were absent from the meeting, you convey only a limited amount of information. More to the point, you might convey different information to different readers, because *several* represents one quantity to one person, another quantity to another person. "Six members were absent from the meeting" leaves no room for interpretation or doubt.

In our previous book, *The Write Way,* we call concrete language "the language of control" because concrete language enables the writer to control the message, whereas abstract language allows the reader to control the message.

In many cases, this will be of no great moment, but even if it isn't, the habit of using specific language is a good one to cultivate. Concrete language conveys a more forceful, more interesting impression.

Let's look again at the passage we used as an illustration in our discussion of the Second Principle:

> Research and available data about employee performance indicates that there is a relationship between an employee's frame of mind and safe work behavior. It is now more fully recognized that if an employee has personal and family problems on his or her mind, their ability to concentrate on their work can be impacted. One area that is particularly distractful [sic] to employees is erratic or unusual behavior of children, especially teenaged youngsters.

The paragraph is enfeebled by generalities:

- "indicates"
- "relationship between an employee's frame of mind and safe work behavior"
- "safe work behavior"
- "can be impacted"

A discerning reader wonders, "What does *indicates* mean? Does the research prove the relationship, or just "point to" some ill-defined conclusion? What kind of relationship? How can the worker's ability to concentrate be impacted? And what does *impacted* really mean?"

Our revision is simpler, shorter, and more specific:

> Research has shown that workers with personal problems are more likely to have accidents. This is especially true when a problem involves the employee's teenage child.

For most of us, generalities fall easily off the tongue, but specifics require thought. Therefore, overreliance on generalities is the lazy way to write. To make your writing come alive by using more concrete language, we have these suggestions:

- Never use an abstract word or phrase when you can think of a concrete one that is appropriate. *Seven* is stronger than *several; ninety-three years old* is better than *aged; has heart disease and diabetes* is better than *in ill health;* and so on.
- Learn to respect words that represent things you can see, touch, count, taste, smell—men and women, chairs, houses, spaghetti and meatballs, and the like.
- Describe what happened: "The Boy Scout helped an old woman across the street" is better than "The Boy Scout did a good deed."
- Show, rather than tell.

The Eighth Principle: Watch your language.

Words mean things. You can no more write well without using words well than a composer can create a symphony without understanding rhythm and harmony. Good writers know that connotations are often more important than definitions, and that the true meaning of a word or phrase is the effect it has on readers.

The chief executive of a large company wrote to the company's customers a letter in which this sentence appeared: "We seek to contribute to the so-called quality of life in our community by providing quality health care at affordable cost." *So-called* quality of life? *So-called* has a clearly negative connotation: The executive implied that the quality of life in the community was low. Surely the executive intended no such implication.

Words can have powerful emotional effects. It is possible for a survey to show that a majority of people oppose "social welfare" while another survey, using a similar sample of the population, reveals that most favor "aid to poor people." The contradiction is understandable: *Social welfare* evokes a negative vision to many people, but few Americans lack compassion for the poor.

In 1987 and 1988, Congress and the nation debated the question of whether the United States should provide military support to the Nicaraguan Contras. Opponents adopted the slogan, "Give peace a chance"—a strong emotional appeal. Proponents had nothing similar. Someone suggested that if the proponents had used "Give freedom a chance" as their rallying cry, their message might have swayed more people to their point of view.

Several basic tools can help you use words effectively. A standard dictionary is, of course, essential. Owning an up-to-date dictionary is important because of the thousands of words that have come into the language in recent years and because definitions and usages are constantly changing.

A good dictionary attempts to give all possible meanings of a word, but it is not always a reliable guide to preferred usage. For that, a usage dictionary or manual is needed. Several excellent ones are available.

If you want to know, for example, when to use *on behalf of* rather than *in behalf of,* or if you'd like to know whether *importantly* or *important* is preferred in "most important(ly)," a usage manual will have the answer. Often the authors of usage manuals arrive at their judgments in consultation with panels of writers and other respected professionals. For this reason, a usage manual is neither pedantic nor excessively permissive. Comments of panel members may be included with many entries, and they make interesting reading.

For the serious writer or logophile, various specialized dictionaries are available. These include dictionaries with word histories, dictionaries of slang, dictionaries of foreign terms, reverse dictionaries, and many others.

Another tool that will help you use words more effectively is a thesaurus. A thesaurus will give a list of synonyms from which you can choose one that might say what you want to say. An even better tool is a book that gives different connotations of synonymous words. The entry for *misery*, for example, might list *agony, anguish, distress, passion,* and *torture*. A discussion of connotations would describe the subtle differences among these synonyms. This is a tool for discriminating writers.

Beyond learning the precise meanings of words and being aware of their connotations, these suggestions can help you to use language more effectively:

• **Use jargon, technical terms, and slang sparingly if at all.** Jargon is language peculiar to a particular group, business, profession, or activity. In its place, jargon is appropriate and easily understood. Similarly, technical language is appropriate in technical documents. Neither should appear in material written for general audiences. Slang can be effective, but only in very informal writing.

• **Avoid most euphemisms.** A euphemism is a "pleasant" term for something that is supposedly unpleasant. Euphemisms may seem harmless, and many are. But to the extent that a euphemism conveys incorrect information, it can interfere with clear understanding. To us it seems vaguely insulting to readers to use a term such as "passed away" for *died*—as though they are emotionally unable to accept the reality of death.

- **Avoid most clichés.** Earlier in the book we debunked the myth that all clichés are bad. Now we remind you that we do not condone the frequent, purposeless use of worn-out phrases. When you are tempted to use some clever expression that you've read recently, take the time to come up with something a bit fresher.
- **Suit the words to the reader, the subject, and the purpose of the writing.** Different audiences and different purposes require different styles. Contractions, personal pronouns, and other informalities are acceptable for many kinds of writing, but others require a more formal style.

The Ninth Principle: Help the reader.

An often-repeated axiom is that communication is a two-way street. But clear communication is the responsibility of the writer, not the reader. The writer must therefore give the reader all possible help in understanding what is written.

Everything we have said to this point leads to the Ninth Principle. Brevity, simplicity, proper word usage, and other writing techniques do indeed contribute to clarity of style. Beyond these, the two most important contributors to clarity are emphasis and cohesiveness.

Emphasis

Writing and speaking are different media of communication. An important difference between them is the methods available for emphasis. Emphasis in speaking comes from gestures, inflection, facial expressions, pauses, and "body language." Emphasis in writing can be achieved through the use of italics, boldface type, underlining, and exclamation points. There are, however, more subtle ways to emphasize.

One of the best ways to emphasize is to use the right word order. Words and ideas that you want to emphasize should come near the end of the sentence. Contrast two versions of the thought expressed in the first sentence of this paragraph:

> One of the best ways to emphasize is *to use the right word order.*
>
> *Using the right word order* is one of the best ways to emphasize.

The first version makes the point more emphatically than the second by putting the most important idea, "the right word order," in the latter part of the sentence. Considering the sentence in context, we find that its first part, "One of the best ways to emphasize," serves as a transition from the previous paragraph. Many writers construct most of their sentences that way. The technique not only puts the emphasis where they want it, but it also facilitates the flow of ideas. Their paragraphs are composed of sentences in which the less important information or the idea at the beginning of each sentence ties in with the more important idea—anything new that they want to introduce—at the end of the preceding one. Note how the following sentences relate in that way:

> There are, however, *better ways to emphasize.* One of the best is *to use the right word order.* Using the right word order helps the writer *to ensure continuity.*

The important idea in the first sentence is *better ways to emphasize.* It flows to *one of the best,* which is the less important idea in the second. New information, *to use the right word order,* is introduced in the latter part of the second sentence. The third sentence continues the process by repeating the old idea, *using the right word order,* at the beginning and introducing the new thought, *to ensure continuity,* at the end. Rewriting the three sentences to reverse the word order, we get:

> *Better ways to emphasize* are available, however. *Using the right word order* is one of the best. *Continuity* is ensured by using the right word order.

The difference between the versions is striking. The first is smooth and natural, the second, choppy and stilted. The first puts the emphasis where it belongs; the second allows each thought to tail off into nothing like the outermost ring of ripples on a pond.

The same technique is used to emphasize ideas and information in clauses within a sentence. For example:

> Anyone who wants to write well must learn *how to use emphasis,* and emphasis is more than *italics or underlining;* of course, such devices are useful, but a skillful writer favors *subtler techniques.*

In each clause of that sentence, the new or important idea is in the latter part. Compare it with:

> *Learning to use emphasis* is essential to anyone who wants to write well, and *italics and underlining* are not all there is to emphasis; *subtler techniques* are favored by skillful writers, even though such devices as italics and underlining are useful.

In long sentences, elements to be emphasized are often placed immediately before punctuation marks. This helps keep long sentences from getting out of control.

Another technique for adding dramatic emphasis is unnecessary repetition. Example:

The company must invest more in research in order *to* develop new products, *to* compete in the marketplace, and *to* provide a better return to investors.

That sentence could be written this way:

The company must invest more in research in order to develop new products, compete in the marketplace, and provide a better return to investors.

The simple repetition of *to* in first version subtly emphasizes each of the three reasons for the company's need to invest more in research.

Dramatic emphasis can also be added by departing from the normal (subject, verb, object) word order. For example, "There on the floor in plain sight was the ring of keys I had been searching for"; "Down the street strode the friendly giant."

A good speaker emphasizes by using pauses. Pauses are of varying duration, and their effect on the listener varies with their duration. A good writer can get much the same effect with punctuation marks. Different punctuation marks indicate pauses of different duration, or "strength," and they have different effects on the reader.

A comma, for example, indicates a short pause and relatively minor emphasis, which accounts for the fact that commas are considered optional more often than are other marks of punctuation. In some sentences the addition of a comma where none is required gives subtle emphasis to a thought. Compare:

In some sentences the addition of a comma where none is required gives subtle emphasis to a thought.

In some sentences, the addition of a comma where none is required gives subtle emphasis to a thought.

In the second version, the emphasis on *in some sentences* is slightly greater than in the first.

What we tend to think of as punctuation rules are sometimes violated for the sake of emphasis. In conventional usage, a comma before a conjunction is not recommended if a dependent clause follows. For example: "The company began a research program last year and brought several new products to market." Some writers would put a comma before *and* in order to show that the new products were the result of the research program, not merely coincidental to it. Whether using the comma in that way can be justified is debatable. Using a comma before *and* would change the second part of the compound predicate into an independent clause by implying a subject—*it* or *the company*.

If emphasis is the goal, a dash is the better choice: "The company began a research program last year—and brought several new products to market."

Achieving cohesiveness

One of the most common writing problems we see in the work of seminar participants is lack of cohesiveness. They often show samples of writing that just doesn't "hang together" even though the individual sentences may be well constructed. Writing cohesive sentences is relatively easy. Writing cohesive paragraphs is a little harder, and writing cohesive passages consisting of several paragraphs is harder still. Writing cohesively is easier if the writer understands grammar, punctuation, sentence structure, and transitions; but thoughtful attention must be given to content and sequence. To write copy that hangs together, you must consider how each element (word, phrase, sentence, paragraph) relates to and affects other elements, especially those that immediately follow and precede it. The objective is to lead the reader smoothly from one sentence to the next and from one paragraph to the next.

Consider, for example, the preceding paragraph. The first sentence, "One of the most common writing problems we see in the work of seminar participants is lack of cohesiveness," establishes the topic of the paragraph. The second sentence defines the term and restates the problem. From there the reader is led smoothly and naturally to the final sentence, which serves as a transition into the next paragraph.

Notice that the third, fourth, and fifth sentences all begin with *writing* and the fourth contains an independent clause that begins with *writing*. This repetition helps to tie the sentences together and in that way contributes to the paragraph's cohesiveness.

We constructed that paragraph carefully to illustrate the principle of cohesiveness. In most writing, however, the cohesive forces are not so easily identified; but they are there. Consider the following paragraph from *Writing to Learn*, by William Zinsser. As you read the excerpt, notice how the author leads you gently along by making each sentence relate to the one that precedes it:

> In January I rented a cap and gown and received my dubious B.A. and went out into the world. Several months later I got a job with the *New York Herald Tribune* and began what has turned out to be a career of trying to write clearly and—as an editor and a teacher—to help other people to write clearly. I've become a clarity nut. I've also become a logic nut. I'm far less preoccupied than I once was with individual words and their picturesque roots and origins and with the various fights over which new ones should be admitted to the language. These are mere skirmishes at the edge of the battlefield; I will no longer man the ramparts to hurl back such barbarisms as "hopefully."

Another path to cohesiveness is the effective use of transitions. A transition is a sort of signal that tells the reader to expect a change of subject, a continuation, an example, or a modification of a previous statement. A transition makes reading easier by preparing the reader to assimilate new information.

Examples of common transitions include *however, for example, nevertheless, as a result, in addition, consequently, in summary, finally, in other words, at the same time, furthermore, to illustrate,* and *on the other hand.* Many of these simple transitions are overused, and time spent in thinking of better ones might be well spent. Often a full sentence makes a good transition. The final sentence in a paragraph can lead smoothly to the opening of the next.

Overused, transitions can make writing tiresome. Well selected and skillfully placed, transitions contribute to clarity and cohesiveness. Your ear and sense of logic should tell you when a transition is needed to make your writing cohesive.

Cohesiveness is the product of a sensitive ear and an orderly mind. Most good writers make little *conscious* effort to achieve it. The student, however, can benefit from paying more attention to the things that make writing hang together and in the process can order the mind and train the ear.

The Tenth Principle: Train the ear.

Writing is at once a visual and an aural medium. Although not all writing is intended to be read aloud, most good writing can *be read aloud with no detrimental effect. It is important, therefore, for anyone who wants to write well to train the ear to recognize the good and bad aural qualities.*

Good writing has a quality variously described as "rhythm," "symmetry," "balance," "cadence," and "style." Whatever you want to call it, this quality is really "ear appeal." What it amounts to is, good writing *sounds* good. True, writing communicates visually; but it also communicates aurally, which is to say the reader "hears" through the mind's ear what he sees on the paper. For this reason, the often-advanced argument that the ear is not a good guide to the placement of commas is specious.

The lack of ear appeal in writing is easy to discern, but defining the factors that produce it is another matter. Many of the principles discussed in this book, such as emphasis, cohesion, word choice, parallelism, relate to how writing sounds. The writer who pays attention to these principles usually produces writing with ear appeal. Conversely, writing that sounds good usually follows the principles of good writing. Beyond that, however, a sense of rhythm will tell a skillful writer that some words just don't belong together.

To illustrate, suppose we had written, "The reader's mind's ear hears what he sees on the paper." The two possessives together and the juxtaposition of *ear* and *hears* create an unpleasant combination of sounds. Instead, we wrote, "The reader 'hears' through the mind's ear what he sees on the paper." You'll agree there's quite a difference in the sounds.

Punctuation and sentence structure contribute to ear appeal because readers tend to hear as well as see punctuation. Periods, colons, and dashes create dramatic pauses that contribute to rhythm and balance, characteristics that relate more to sound than sight. Variety in sentence length and style makes writing more appealing to hear and read. Conversely, a succession of sentences of about the same length and style is offensive to the ear and boring to the mind.

Some teachers urge their students to try writing poetry as a way to develop a better sense of rhythm. More practical advice, however, is to read aloud now and then. Try reading from articles in *National Geographic* and *Smithsonian* magazines or stories by Ernest Hemingway. Above all, read some of your own writing aloud or have someone read it to you. You'll be able to tell whether it has ear appeal.

Some closing thoughts on the craft of writing

Everyone loves to write; few love to revise. But the best writers are the writers who have the discipline to revise and revise and revise. If we had to point to a single difference between professionals and amateurs, it would be that amateurs are likely to be satisfied with one or two drafts; professionals rarely are. Anyone who is satisfied with first-draft writing is either extraordinarily talented or has low standards. Ernest Hemingway, who was extraordinarily talented and had the highest of standards, once told an interviewer that he rewrote the ending to *A Farewell to Arms* thirty-nine times. Samuel Johnson said, "What is written without effort is in general read without pleasure."

Good writing always benefits from good editing. A sentence that seems to the writer to be clear as the mountain air, a phrase turned to perfection, an analogy that dramatizes the point, a word that expresses a thought precisely—all these might look different to another pair of eyes. Some writers dislike having anyone tamper with their work, but an editor can be the writer's best friend.

Writing without thinking is impossible, but some people try to do it. Most of the examples you read in our discussion of syntax were the result of the writer's failure to think about what was really said. Clear writing is inevitably the result of clear thinking. It follows, then, that learning to write better forces one to learn to think better.

Once you have committed your thoughts to paper, they tend to take on a certain permanence. For better or worse, they represent you. The care and effort you put into what you write may be evident in them. That in itself is reason enough to write as well as you can.

We have offered you some guiding principles. In our work we have found these principles to be sound. If you apply them diligently, they will support you like a rock.

Answers

The difference a word makes (page 115)

1. *a* **2.** *b* **3.** *a* **4.** *b* **5.** *a* **6.** *b* **7.** *b* **8.** *a* **9.** *b* **10.** *a*

11. *b* **12.** *a* **13.** *b* **14.** *a* **15.** *b* **16.** *a* **17.** *a* **18.** *a* **19.** *b*

20. *a* **21.** *a* **22.** *b* **23.** *a* **24.** *b* **25.** *b* **26.** *a* **27.** *a* **28.** *b*

29. *a* **30.** *a* **31.** *a* **32.** *b* **33.** *b* **34.** *a* **35.** *b*

A comedy of errors (page 121)

1. Sir Rodney might be sweating because he realizes that his creator has messed up the sign, which should read: SLAUGHTER AT **ITS** BEST. *It's* is a contraction, not a possessive pronoun.

2. *Less* means "not so much" and refers to amount and quantity. *Fewer* means "not so many" and refers to number, things that are countable, such as the candles on a cake. ". . . by using **fewer** and **fewer** candles on your cake" is preferable.

3. Lucy is perpetrating an apostrophe catastrophe. She is trying out for the **girls'** (or **girls**) basketball team, because more than one girl plays on the squad.

4. Even a senator should know that one ends a quotation with **end quote**, not *unquote*.

5. **Millennium,** not *millenium*. The percentage of instances in which this word is misspelled makes *millennium* very probably the most misspelled word in the English language.

6. Larsen E. Pettifogger should be urging his client to crawl ten feet **farther,** not further. *Farther* indicates concrete, physical distance and means "at a greater distance," while *further* describes abstract distance and means "more, to a greater extent."

7. It is the **enormousness** of the universe that turns on Carl Sagan. *Enormousness* and *enormity* both denote largeness, but *enormity* is reserved for the idea of wickedness and *enormousness* for objects and concepts involving great size.

8. "It's okay for you and **me,**" *me* being an object of the preposition *for.*

9. **I,** not *myself.* The suspicious-looking *need* is actually correct because it agrees with the nearer pronoun, *I.*

10. A hose **lies** ("reposes") there, not lays there. In "Bloom County" Opus exclaimed, "Those butchers! Come in . . . lay down . . . ," and even the know-it-all Calvin, of "Calvin and Hobbes," messed up this verb pair when he said, "If the rest of you lay low, we can take turns going to school, and no one will be the wiser."

11. In "with you and I," the pronouns are both objects of the preposition *with.* Thus, *I* should be **me.**

12. The "Wizard of Id" king is not much of a wizard of idiom here. Standard English speakers use **different from** before a noun or noun expression, not *different than.* After all, nobody would say, "A differs than B."

13. "There **are** no four-letter words in it." "Four-letter words" is a plural subject that must take a plural verb, *are.*

14. A rare double boo-boo. Most obvious is the double negative "none . . . neither," which is a no-no. Less obvious is "there's none." Because the announcer is talking about the fleas collectively and not individually, we would argue that the correct form is "there **are** none."

15. ". . . where my very first sweetheart and **I** . . ." *I* is the subject of the verb *carved* and must therefore be cast in the nominative case.

Moreover, the pronoun designating the speaker should come after, not before, any third- or second-person references.

16. To keep demonstrative pronouns and the nouns in agreement, standard English speakers say, **that kind** or **those kinds.**

17. The speaker really wants a wine that will **complement** ("complete") the mystery meat, assuming that the wine can't talk and say, "Hey, great meat!"

18. Puristically, it's **annoy,** not *aggravate. Annoy* means "to irritate," *aggravate* "to make worse."

19. Of course Nancy can sit *on* Sluggo's lap, but she should have asked, "**May** I sit on your lap?"

20. "I may just get **nauseated.**" If you say or write, "I'm nauseous today," your listener may shoot back, "How honest of you to admit it." On the model *poisonous/poisoned, nauseous* means "causing nausea," while **nauseated** means "experiencing nausea."

21. The Id peasant is actually pointing to a **lectern,** not a podium. We stand on a small, portable platform called a podium (from a Greek root for "foot"), but we rest our notes on and speak from an item of furniture called a lectern (from a Latin root for "read").

22. ". . . Contract employees such as **you**." *Yourself* is a reflexive pronoun and seldom used in other contexts.

23. **Media** (Latin singular *-um,* plural *-a*) is the standard form of *medium*. Mediums are practitioners who communicate with the dead.

24. General Halftrack (who, in the panel, has a smile on his face) is **eager,** not anxious, to take rifle practice. Both *eager* and *anxious* mean "desiring to do something," but underlying *anxious* is a hint of apprehension.

25. ". . . Better than **we** [are]." In such adverb clauses of comparison, the verb *are* is understood, requiring the pronoun to be cast in the nominative case. We'd also prefer ". . . **as if** [or **as though**] she's better than we are."

26. Because *PIN* is an initialism standing for "personal identifi-

cation number," "PIN number" is a redundancy, like "ATM machine," "ISBN number," "MAC card," "HIV virus," and "RSVP please."

27. *To whither* occupies a prominent place in the files of the Department of Redundancy Department. Because **whither** means "to where," *to whither* is repetitive, known in the language business as a pleonasm. *Whither* is much like *whence,* which means "from where."

Also the verb in the panel should be **dost** or **doth,** not *doest.*

28. Honchos by definition are "head," so "head honcho" is a redundancy, as may well be "poor peon."

29. The Woodley family consists of more than one Woodley, so the plural possessive form is "the **Woodleys'** yard." In the same comic strip we have also seen a panel that reads, "It's really time to leave for the O'Reilly's party."

30. More apostrophe catastrophe. While *Women's* and *Misses'* are plural possessives, *Junior's* is a singular possessive. **Juniors'** is what was meant.

31. The senator is using foul language here. *Insure* means "to provide or procure insurance for." **Ensure,** the better word here, means "to make certain."

32. Rather than effecting ("bringing about") an English accent, the Peachy kid is **affecting** ("pretending to have") that manner of speech.

33. Both a subjective-verb disagreement and a jarring shift from the first to the third person have sent this sentence hurtling toward oblivion. Vastly more proper would have been "I, Cutter John, . . . now **find myself** . . ."

34. Snoopy has typed a dangling modifier because the introductory phrase, "When mixing dog food in a bowl," doesn't modify anything in the main clause. Better would have been "When mixing dog food in a bowl, you may put in the water first or add it last."

35. The *only* is misplaced here and seems to suggest that the young hunter should only *shoot* what he is going to eat, not stab or

cage it. Clearer would have been "**Shoot only** what you're gonna eat."

36. "The reason . . . is because . . ." is both redundant, because *because* is embedded in *reason,* and structurally shoddy. The *is* should be followed by a noun clause, "**that** you never get the ball in the basket . . ."

37. Little Calvin is dangling his participle in public. Calvin, not the rocks, is crossing the rift. The most graceful revision of the second sentence is "As I cross the rift, I note that the rocks change color."

38. Because B.D. and Boopsie are the only two people in the car, they should use the comparative, not the superlative, form of the adjective and exclaim, even in the heat of passion, "It was **harder** on me."

39. Because the infinitive *to symbolize* is followed by four objects, the sentence should read, "Four red roses to symbolize Mike, Liz, April, and **me**."

40. *Farther* represents physical distance, *further* abstract distance. But it may be too much to expect little Dennis to say, "If the stork had landed two houses **farther,** . . ."

41. Because *the Muzak wars* is a plural subject, Zonker should ask, "How **go** the Muzak wars today?"

42. Another example of double trouble: Although it is probably unrealistic to ask someone Nancy's age to employ the subjunctive mood, the proper usage for conditions contrary to fact following the verb *to wish* is "I wish I **were** better looking."

It is also a bit much to ask Sluggo to have control of "one of those people," one of the most difficult constructions to master. Because the adjective clause modifies *people,* the sentence should read, "Maybe you're one of those people who **are** beautiful inside."

43. Yet another two-time loser: Alexander's first comment contains an illogical comparison. Because Dagwood can't do something more than he himself can do it, he orders "more toppings than anyone **else** in the world."

Second, the vat of toppings comes from the **Pizzeria**.

44. "I agree with **whoever** is speaking." *Whoever* is the subject of the verb *is*. The entire noun clause, "whoever is speaking," is the object of the preposition *with*.

45. "For **a while**." *Awhile* is an adverb, as in "Can you stay awhile?" *A while* is the article *a* and the noun *while*, which is used as the object of a preposition.

46. The roots of **astronaut** literally mean "star sailor." Here the corrector herself (or at least her artist) needs correction.

47. "The trick is to try **to** take a book without waking up Duffy." The infinitive, "to take a book," is the object of the verb *try*.

48. It's the accounts of other people. Hence, the phrase should read ". . . from other **people's** accounts."

49. This is a classic example of a dangling modifier. The introductory prepositional phrase has nothing to modify in the main clause, making it appear as though the keys have sent their last child off to college. One possible revision: "With their last child off to college, the Nest Heads revoke the keys to the mini van."

50. Trust us: The joyriding canines are **careering** through the neighborhood. The primary meaning of *careen* is "to cause (a boat) to lean over on one side," while that of the verb *career* is "to go at top speed, in a headlong manner."

The ultimate spelling quiz (page 141)

The total is zero. That's right: All of the words in the list are spelled correctly. If you just happened to circle some of the words, compare your vision of each word with each spelling given. That way you'll go a long way toward taming some of your personal spelling demons.

Punctuation teasers (page 154)

1. A clever dog knows it's master.
2. Call me, fool, if you wish.
3. Woman—without her, man is nothing.

4. I saw a man-eating lobster.

5. Mary, Jane, and I went to see the latest Brad Pitt movie.

6. The butler stood at the door and called the guests' names.

7. Other than that, one thought he was not there.

8. Anne Boleyn kept her head up defiantly; an hour after, she was beheaded.

9. Every lady in this land
Hath twenty nails: upon each hand
Five, and twenty on hand and feet,
And this is true without deceit.

10. There should be more space between "ham" and "and" and "and" and "eggs."

11. That that is, is. That that is not, is not. Is not that it? It is.

12. Mary, where John had had "had," had had "had had." Had "had had" had the teacher's approval, Mary would have been correct.

Index